GLOUCESTERSHIRE

WITHIN LIVING MEMORY

Compiled from contributions gathered
by members of the
Gloucestershire Federation of WIs.

Published jointly by
Countryside Books, Newbury
and the GFWI, Gloucester

First published 1996

COUNTRYSIDE BOOKS
3 Catherine Road
Newbury, Berkshire

ISBN 1 85306 409 2

Front cover photograph shows a threshing machine engine at
Packhurst Farm, Edge c.1920

Back cover photograph shows the Fairford butcher's van in the mid 1930s.

Produced through MRM Associates Ltd., Reading
Printed by Woolnough Bookbinding Ltd., Irthlingborough

CONTENTS

Gloucestershire
N
Herefs.
Worcs.
Tewkesbury
Stanway
Chipping Campden
R. Evenlode
Stow-on-the Wold
Oxon.
Newent
May Hill
Forest of Dean
Gloucester
Cheltenham
Seven Springs
R. Windrush
R. Leach
R. Coln
R. Churn
Coleford
Lydney
Monmouth.
Sharpness Canal
Stroudwater Canal
Gloucester & Sharpness Canal
R. Frome
Stroud
Thames & Severn Canal
Cirencester
Berks.
Thames Head
Tetbury
R. Thames
Berkeley
Dursley
R. Little Avon
R. Severn
R. Wye
Thornbury
Wilts.
Badminton
R. Frome
Dodington
R. Avon
Bristol
Somerset
GFWI

Foreword

"The days of our age are three score years and ten" (*Psalm 90*)

1900 – 1970 A time of unprecedented change

People are rarely, if ever, conscious that they are living in revolutionary times but in fact, those born at the start of this century have done just that. 1919 was the beginning of a great movement – though from the perspective of today's world, it was a small beginning. A child in the 1930s enjoyed playing with marbles and conkers, and the decade witnessed every weekday with its own rigidly ordered timetable of domestic work. A woman's life was almost completely circumscribed by the home, all day and every day. The 1950s was a golden age to some, to others a time of austerity sandwiched between the heroics of wartime and the cultural revolution of the 1960s.

Since the Second World War the village as a self-contained community has almost certainly died. We no longer know everyone else within the parish or within walking distance, nor do we enjoy the delights of local dialect; going to bed early to economise on lamp oil and coal; washing in cold water from pump or well; eating cold ham for breakfast or going without; or finding our way along deserted lanes in the dark and enjoying it ... especially if courting! Improvements in education and transport, town and country planning, television and an avalanche of domestic gadgets, together with telecommunications have destroyed village life – a casualty of progress no less.

During all these years Gloucestershire has made an outstanding contribution to such progress, especially in the field of transport – bicycles, motor cycles, trains, aircraft and agricultural machinery.

Contributors have derived a sense of achievement and it is hoped that all will now find enjoyment in reading this fascinating and often humorous social history covering the Wolds, the Forest and the Vales which

"take us back to Gloucestershire, most glorious land of all"

(words of the late Private Ivor Gurney, Gloucestershire Regiment)

Audrey Fielding,
County Chairman

Acknowledgements

A hearty thanks to both fellow members and friends who took up the challenge to reminisce and forward material and photographs for this rare enchantment. We were delighted to accept contributions from two Avon WIs, Falfield and Almondsbury, members of the Gloucestershire Federation prior to Local Government reorganisation in 1974. To Hermione Thornton (Larkhay) a special thanks for the superb line drawings; and to the many gentlemen whose tales ensured that no aspect of life in glorious Gloucestershire was forgotten, a big thank you. It most certainly would not have been the same without them!

Sadly, for reasons of space, it was impossible to include every contribution, but without exception, all were of great value in recreating Gloucestershire 'within living memory'.

Carole Bevan and Jennie Robinson
Co-ordinators

TOWN & COUNTRY LIFE

Some Towns and Villages Remembered

It is not so long since the traffic on our streets was horse-drawn, or since a child's way to school could be lightened by the smell of new bread from the village bakery and the ring of the blacksmith's hammer at the smithy. Here are just a few memories of times past in town and village – of squire and parson, of political pranks, of shops long gone but not forgotten, of those nicknames everyone seemed to have.

Cheltenham Memories

'Cheltenham was both beautiful and fashionable by the time the 20th century arrived. Well dressed couples frequented the tree-lined Promenade, sometimes accompanied by Nurse pushing their baby in its high-slung perambulator.

Later the town was inhabited, at the high class end, ie the Georgian terraces of Lansdown and the Park, by retired colonels and their ladies from the Indian Raj. They were accustomed to being waited on by many Indian servants, they were total snobs and looked upon servants as a divine right. They sneered at the lower classes (I experienced this whilst working as a librarian in the Promenade during the late 1930s. Some of them could not carry home their chosen library books and these were later delivered to them). Most of them were not well-off but depended on army pensions. Later Cheltenham acquired a new maxim, "Poor, Proud and Pretty". The town was certainly pretty – it had many floral gardens to delight the eye of the visitor. Montpellier Gardens had its bandstand, in use during the 1920s and 1930s, also a First World War tank on display. Opposite is the Rotunda building, an earlier watering place, which is at one end of the Georgian shopping crescent famous for its caryatid pillars – carvings of women in Greek dress. At the top of the Promenade is the elegant Queen's Hotel in front of which, during my childhood, were two field guns brought back from the Crimea and mounted on stone bases. The bases are still there but the guns and tank were melted down to make weapons for the

Second World War, as were the Victorian iron railings which fronted many houses. The Queen's looks down on the stately, tree-lined Promenade with its long gardens, the fountain of Neptune and elegant shops including Cavendish House, now part of the House of Fraser Group. Opposite the Queen's are the well-cared for Imperial Gardens on which once stood the Winter Gardens, a glass-roofed replica of the Crystal Palace in London. I was taken there as a child to see amateur drama performances and the silent cinema. This building was taken down at the outbreak of the 1939 war as it was thought to be too attractive to enemy bombers.

Up and down the High Street were shops of all descriptions, between the wars – many shoe shops, grocers (International and Melia's spring to mind as well as the local Gloucester Dairy and Creamery), butchers, bakers, fishmongers, chemists, jewellers. The tea shops were sheer delight; the Cadena Cafe was one which smelled wonderfully of the coffee they sold in the shop. Department stores such as E. L. Ward, a family firm, were in the centre of town and the Co-operative Store at the end of the Strand. There were about six banks; Lloyds, being the oldest and most famous, was built on the site of the old Assembly Rooms. The Georgian frontage was retained, but the inside was much more practical and access was through revolving glass doors.

Cheltenham had many hotels to accommodate visitors to the festivals and to the races. The racecourse is well outside the town but until recent days the hotel accommodation was only in the town itself. Some of the High Street hotels had been coaching houses, particularly the Plough Hotel which until recently retained its coaching arch leading from the High Street to the yard where the passengers alighted and the horses were stabled. The Plough Hotel is alas no more, having given way to the modern Regent Arcade with its shops and restaurants and its now famous fish musical clock which delights the children. Other High Street hotels, the Royal, the Palace and the Fleece (all now demolished) had a yard behind them which was used as a terminus for country buses. This was convenient for country shoppers who could take a little refreshment whilst waiting for the bus to take them home. This practice continued into the second half of the century, when the motor car became popular and the bus services declined.'

'I came to Cheltenham in 1925 when I was three years old, with my parents and baby sister, when my father became the organist at the Palace cinema in the High Street. He left when talkies came in, in 1928.

We lived in Courtenay Street, in St Paul's, and early memories include cows being driven along the street to the nearby abattoir, and the dripping cake man who cycled round, ringing his bell, on Friday mornings, not to mention the coalman with his horse-drawn cart, shouting "A shilling a hundred", who would empty one of his sacks into the coal-shute in front of our front door, and the Walls man on his bicycle with "Stop Me and Buy One" written on the sides of his container. You could buy a Snofrute (iced lolly) for 1d and a choc-ice for 2d. The baker from Mr Conn's bakery was a jolly man who let us ride on his cart. There wasn't much traffic, so it was quite safe to play with our hoops or tops in the road, depending on the season, and hopscotch on the pavements, but we lost an awful lot of marbles down the drains in the gutters!

After dark, when we were a little older, we played chalk-chases, using chalk marks on various surfaces so that the following "trackers" would be able to rendezvous with us later. As only one boy in our road had any roller skates, we used to queue to borrow them from him, and the child with the cricket bat was always made "captain".

Until the war, most Sunday school treats took the form of a trip to the pleasure ground at Bishop's Cleeve to ride on the slides and swingboats, followed by tea at long trestle tables, consisting mainly of jam doughnuts. There was also an annual procession around St Paul's parish, led by a band and ending with a service outside the church on the lawns at Whitsun. Guides and Scouts held an annual Jamboree in Pittville Park with fire-building and tent-pitching competitions, as well as lighting bonfires on Leckhampton Hill and a joint camp fire in the Town Hall each year, and of course we all wore our uniforms to school on Empire Day (May 24th).

Houses and streets in many parts of Cheltenham were gas lit, and I remember the excitement and controversy over whether to use the blue sodium or the yellow lights in 1937 or thereabouts. There was roller-skating at Montpellier Park, trams in the High Street, and a tripe shop in Bennington Street, usually with a black cat in the window. Dowty House was a boys' orphanage, the

Elms was a workhouse, but later turned into the maternity hospital, and you could watch the Cricket Festival free if you stood by the railings of the Gentleman's College. Chimney sweeps were a familiar sight and charabancs went so slowly up Leckhampton Hill you could actually beat them by running alongside – but they got to Birdlip all right. And the Cheltenham Flyer, which ran from St James' station! (Alas, no more, like the GWR Malvern Road station.) The only trip I made on it was magic, but not exactly smooth! The Hunt set off each Boxing Day from the Queen's Hotel, the band played on summer evenings in the bandstand in Imperial Gardens, the audience reclining in deck chairs, tea dances were held on Wednesdays in the upstairs Boots' Cafe, and at weekends at the Cadena Cafe in the Promenade. I also remember the firemen cleaning their engine each weekend at the old station in St James' Square next to the synagogue and letting me ring their bell as a treat.'

Guiting Power Village Life

'My father ran the village stores at Guiting Power. He would cycle around the neighbouring villages on certain days and call regularly on people to get their orders. These would be put up next day and delivered the same or following day by pony and cart, then by van in the early 1940s.

We were fortunate in having a cold water tap in the house; most people had to go out into the street and collect water from various pumps around the village, the water having initially been pumped up to a reservoir from a spring. Electricity came to the village about 1950 and at the time of the Coronation in 1953 there were two or three televisions in the village.

The shoe repairer, before the war, had a great fascination for us young children, as had the village blacksmith with his varied jobs including shoeing the many horses.

With very few telephones around telegrams were one way of communication. These had to come to the post office, but as the postmistress could not leave the office someone had to be found to deliver them with a small payment being given for delivery.

The village carpenter was also the local undertaker. There was a resident midwife who would cycle round to various villages. There are people still around who were "her babies".

For milk we would go down to the farm dairy with a can or

Stone post office between the wars, the heyday of the village shop.

jug. As children we would watch the cows being milked and the milk would then go to the dairy to be measured into our jugs, with some milk going through the processes for butter making.'

'The halcyon days of my childhood and teenage years have now long gone but my memories, as they say, linger on. At the age of five starting at the village school and on the way there the smell of freshly baked bread coming from the bakehouse and the clang of the blacksmith's hammer on his anvil took my attention. The schoolroom was just one room, half for infants and half for children six to eleven years, with no partition, yet we had some of the finest education and discipline anywhere. Just one schoolmistress and a monitor managed the children (about 40 in all) and the room was heated by a black, round iron tortoise coal stove which in the winter was topped by an enamel pan with water, into which our mid-morning thirds of a pint of milk in their little glass bottles were put to warm. The summer passed with a variety of games. Hoops, hopscotch, tops, all in strict rotation interspersed with singing games.

Sundays were special. Sunday school in the afternoon, then a walk. In the summer we walked around the fields of grass waiting to be cut for hay with giant moon-daisies standing erect and graceful. The fields of golden corn were ablaze with poppies. Along the roadsides you could find cowslips, harebells, quaker grass, scabious, meadow cranesbill and knapweed. High above, larks sang as they rose to the heavens. In winter, hares could be seen chasing from field to field, rabbits nibbled at the young corn, pheasants and partridges searched for any dropped seeds and mice and voles scuttled in the hedgerows looking for berries to fill their larders.

At Christmas the rector gave a party at the rectory. Everyone had new clothes and a present and I shall never forget the sausages on sticks (not having seen them before). Each summer the Sunday school outing was to Porthcawl a trip and excitement never to be forgotten.

The village had two shops, one with a post office, the other with the only telephone that could be used by the public. With the phone in the back of the shop you had to be careful of your conversation as customers were only too keen to listen. This shop sold everything from pins to paraffin and was a real meeting place. In 1938 electricity came to the village, a great boon to all.

At the age of 13 I went to the Technical College in Cheltenham. Again the daily walk to the bus but by now the war news was bad. However, the village hall was open six days a week in the evenings for snooker, darts, reading and a little gossip and we even ran the County library from there weekly. Every three months the books were changed, the new ones being delivered by carrier from the railway station. On alternate Friday evenings there was the village hop (entrance fee 6d) and a whist or beetle drive. Although it was rather a job to see the cards with only oil lamps (the hall had no electricity then), everyone enjoyed themselves. The large coal fire at one end of the room meant you were burning at that end and freezing at the other. Therefore if you wanted to keep warm you were pleased when you lost at whist and you kept your place by the fire. A New Year's social was held every year with all the children from the village taking part and although rationing was in force we always found plenty of refreshments. The village had a good cricket team (all local men) and the ladies had quite a successful hockey team and most of the village followed these teams regularly. A garden fete was held in the manor grounds once a year and the proceeds helped to keep the amenities going.

The war ended. The village school closed, the blacksmith retired, the shop closed and very slowly everything changed.'

TIBBERTON

'The village of Tibberton was very quiet until the 1940s. Until the war there were only 80 houses and all residents worked locally, mostly for the estate which had a great influence on the parish, so everybody knew everybody. The Price family being Unitarians, no pubs were allowed so everyone was sober and talked to one another or drank cider in one another's homes. Mother used to say, "Did you hear that car go past last night? I wonder who that was!" It could only have been one of two people as there were few cars. The parson of Taynton, Irishman Henry Herrick, was very precise and in his car, registration AFH 49, he picked me up for my confirmation. M. P. Price had a car with the number CDF 939.

The Reverend Herrick decided to form a choir and paid 6d each time we attended but for each time that we didn't attend, we owed him 6d. Payment was every six weeks so if we went three times and missed three times, we didn't get anything at all!

My father was an undertaker, There was a bit of competition in the village because Charlie Teague, who lived in the middle of the village and was a great Methodist, was the village undertaker. Grandfather was the estate carpenter but in 1909 decided to go "private", built a carpenter's shop and started business on his own. My father joined him and after his death continued the business. As a carpenter he did a bit of building but thought there to be more money made in undertaking. He regularly got on his bike to go and measure someone up. Before making the coffin, old lady Beet Blewitt was sent to lay the body out. To ensure the box was not too long and too wide, Father would tie the deceased's arms and feet up. He kept a supply of coffin boards – elm for the "cheapo's" and oak for the dear ones.

There being no electricity he couldn't work in the evenings but with no mortuary each job was urgent as there was nowhere to put the body. So, the coffin was made in the kitchen! Many a time he polished and lined by night and when I was a young lad I well remember Father on one occasion saying to me, "You'd better try it for size." I jumped in and he went to put the lid on until Mother shouted, "Don't you put the lid on him, Bert."'

THE FOREST OF DEAN

'I was born in the Forest of Dean. Not today's Forest with its picnic sites and visitors' trails. My Forest was not always an agreeable cradle. It was dominated by the collieries which, in the 1920s, were already feeling the chill winds of depression. My very earliest recollections are hearing the Crump Meadow hooter blowing in the afternoon, bringing my father in off the garden to say, wearily, "Play day again tomorrow, Mother." During the long summer months the coal trade declined for fires were not needed. Colliers were therefore on short time and the method the owners used to tell them when there was no work on the morrow was to blow the hooter – each pit at a pre-determined time. So the next day was a "play day" – a somewhat ironic way to describe short time working. That hooter dominated my childhood as the cold winds of depression headed into the slump of the 1930s. Some weeks only three shifts would be worked – at wages which averaged 7s 9d a shift.

The strike of 1926 went on for nine months and has left bitter memories in the hearts of many old colliers to this day. My most cherished memory of that time was going to Grandad's farm to see the pit ponies. They were brought to the surface during that time; their heads covered in sacking until they gradually became used to the daylight – daylight which some of them had not seen for years. They cantered and galloped, heads tossing, manes flying; it was a sight I can never forget.

Our seaside was Newnham on Severn. At that time there was a decent stretch of sand at the ferry. We walked down the fields from Pleasant Stile carrying our basket of food and drink, our buckets and spades. Parents came too, for the Severn even then was a sly river and when the tide turned it was easy to get cut off. Occasionally, as a great treat, we were taken down on the old GWR rail car, the steam engine puffing its way down through the Forest and into Newnham station with its flower beds ablaze with geraniums and marigolds – and often, even a row of kidney beans!

A great day for all Foresters was Speech House Demonstration in July. This was the day the colliers gathered together at the

Speech House to hear fiery speeches from Union officials; the "gale" money was decided and later distributed to the Free-miners. Then it was all the fun of the fair – steam engines, fairground organs, beer tents, ginger snaps, quack "doctors" with their cure-all medicines, and little sawdust balls on elastic which cost a penny each – and rarely lasted longer than the walk home through the woods as dusk fell.

Dad had a deep bass voice and sang with the local male voice choir for most of his life. Silver and brass bands were also common – every Forest town had at least one. During the summer months there were frequent contests when we all trooped off – a basket of food and drink, of course – to Ruardean or Lydney or Walford. To this day the smell of wet, trodden grass can conjure up the marching bands, the smell of the traction engines, the beer tent, "Martyrs of the Arena" and "See the Conquering Hero Comes!"

Since Cinderford more or less grew up around the ironworks and collieries, it spread gradually up the hillside in a rather haphazard fashion. In the centre of the town was "Hallelujah Tump" (a "tump" in the Forest is a little hillock). Our tump is reputed to have got its name because it was here that the Salvation Army gathered, the lassies in their fetching bonnets shaking their tambourines and singing away "Dare to be a Daniel" – and the men would pile out of the nearby Union pub to join in the singing.

Sunday nights in the summer, after church and chapel, most families would go for a walk along the top of the hill, with its lovely views across the Severn Vale to the distant Cotswolds. Grandad's farm was situated near to Abbotswood and across his fields on Sunday nights would wind a procession of sedate children in their Sunday best, Mums with the baby in a pushchair, Grans and Grandads, arms linked, and the young folk on the lookout for a partner in order to start "courting". We looked forward to Sunday nights and the "monkey parade" as it was known!

Callers at the farm were always welcomed. The gipsies were regulars. Baskets of pegs, bunches of wild daffodils in spring, gaily painted wooden flowers in winter, mushrooms on misty autumn mornings (quite probably picked in Grandad's own fields!). When the days grew colder a frequent visitor was Neddy the shoe black, carrying his box of tricks. He would spend a few nights curled up in the barn, entertaining us by "playing" tunes, using his brushes rather like clappers. Then he would go off on his travels again. After him would come Matty Butler with his knife and scissor-grinding equipment; he also took a night's lodgings in the barn before moving on to Drybrook or Lydbrook.

Harvest times brought an influx of casual labour — mostly the colliers on their "play days". They would work from dawn to dusk for a couple of shillings – and as much of Grandad's cider as it took. The cider was brewed on the farm and, like all cider locally, was popularly known as "stunnem". Grandad brewed a less lethal variety for haymaking and harvest; after all, legless helpers would have been of little use to him or to themselves!

When the last sheaves had been carried to the rickyard on the big waggon fitted with "thripples" to enable full loads to be moved safely along the rutted farm tracks, the colliers' wives and children moved in to glean the fields of the last vestiges of fallen grain. Many a cottage pig and hen would benefit from this unexpected addition to their diet, fattening them up for the inevitable slaughter as Christmas drew nearer.

Wyck Rissington

'The village of Wyck Rissington lies a mile off the A429 between Stow on the Wold and Bourton on the Water.

Until the 1930s it formed the centre of a country estate amounting to some 3,000 acres, dominated by the Hall in its own park. Almost the entire working population lived in the 24 cottages and was employed on the estate.

A large staff was kept both indoors and out and included a butler and footman, eight maids, six gardeners, several coachmen, wheelwrights and ancillary trades. There was also an internal laundry.

The stables were full of horses, including hunters. For the farm work, there were six draught horses managed by a carter, an under-carter and a boy. Many conveyances, such as carriages, broughams, governess carts and dog carts were kept. A horse and cart hauled the household coal from the station. On the farm the corn stacks were built on frames supported by mushroom-capped staddle stones, to make it easier for the farm cats to deal with the rats.

The squire paid for the upkeep of the church out of his own

Wyck Rissington was an estate village until the 1950s.

pocket and only collections for charity were taken. He was one of the first owners of a Rolls-Royce in the district and, when asked the cost by a friend, replied, "I didn't have enough money to buy a suit of clothes out of one thousand pounds."

A fire seriously damaged part of the Hall in 1909. The butler, being awakened by the bell in his pantry ringing violently, despatched one of the young men by bicycle to Stow some three miles away, where he rang the bell and roused the fire brigade.

Her Majesty's Inspectors, afterwards known as the Board of Education Inspectors, constantly expressed themselves favourably impressed with the work and standard of the school, but it closed in 1937 for the centralisation of schools, when there were only seven pupils attending it.

Life after the First World War was hard for the villagers. One old man recalls that he left school at 13 and worked on the estate for 9s a week from 7 am to 5 pm. This was later increased to 25s a week with 6d an hour overtime after 5 pm. A pension was 10s a week. From an early age he went twice a week to the big house, with other children from the village, to have his milk can filled with soup. This had to last for several meals. Most cottagers kept a pig fed on potatoes and meal delivered by horse and cart from the mill. Each pig killed would be shared among neighbours. The keeping of a pig went out some years ago, possibly partly due to changed slaughtering laws.

The absence of a public house encouraged the local cider making industry, and most of the farms had one or two orchards. Equipment for chopping the apples and extracting the juice into a vast vat was brought from a neighbouring village. There was never a shortage of willing helpers, not to mention bystanders, as the communal sampling handbowl was passed around! The orchards no longer exist and only a handful of the old apple trees remain as a reminder.

There was a village shop by the green – later a cartshed and then a fertiliser store – which sold everything from paraffin to groceries and sweets. The shopkeeper was a jack-of-all-trades. He fetched and carried from the railway station (the line closed by Beeching in 1962) in his horse and trap and also did pig-killing, haircutting and many other jobs. When he died local traders brought provisions to the village, first by horse-drawn vehicles and then by vans.

The estate changed hands in 1921, but life continued much as before with the same large staff still employed; the only difference being that the coachmen were replaced by chauffeurs and under-chauffeurs. It was said that the village enjoyed its hey-day in the next ten year period. But it was not to last.

With the Wall Street crash came the depression and the estate in 1929, came on the market again. It was the end of an era. Unable to find a buyer as a desirable country property it was sold to a developer and broken up into numerous lots.

The war followed and the village went into a state of total decline and neglect, with docks, thistles and nettles abounding and it was not until the 1950s that it began to pick up again.

Mains water came to the village about this time. Up till then water had been supplied from the various springs and from a fountain erected to commemorate the Coronation of George V. For baths, water was heated in the copper in the washhouse. Mains sewerage came some 20 years later. Before then sewage was disposed of in a withy bed on one of the farms and in septic tanks. All the cottages had Elsans at the bottom of their gardens. These were emptied at night onto the gardens, which is the secret of how they grew such wonderful vegetables!

Cricket was a serious and favourite pastime up to the 1930s and Wyck Rissington possessed its own team but sadly it lost its cricket pitch in the break-up. Thereafter cricket matches were only played on the green on special occasions, such as the Queen's Silver Jubilee. On one such occasion, "the Colonel" had his arm broken by a demon bowler on a bumpy pitch!'

HUNTLEY

'My father rented a farm, about a mile out of the village, on the Huntley Manor Estate – as did his father before him. It was a mixed farm of about 70 acres and, when I was growing up in the 1920s, he employed two men to help him, but when farming went through a bad patch in the 1930s, they had to go and casual labour was used at busy times such as haymaking, harvesting and fruit picking, and neighbouring farmers helped each other. He kept dairy cows and sold some milk at the door – people collected it each day in cans and left an empty can for the next day. The rest of the milk went to Cadbury's – in churns left at the roadside and collected by lorry. Once or twice he and my mother joined with other farmers on visits to Bournville by special train and a neighbour came to do the evening milking.

We had a cider mill and press, in the covered shed, and one of the jobs for my brother and me to do in the autumn was to pick up the cider apples which had been shaken from the trees – often a cold, wet job but not as cold or unpleasant as picking sugar beet, which the men did. One or two people from the village brought their apples over and made their own cider.

Pheasants were reared on the estate and the keeper came round in the spring wanting broody hens to sit on the eggs at hatching time (the hens were returned later). All the tenant farmers received a brace of pheasants at Christmas time.

We had a village policeman and our house was one of those at which he left a "ticket" when he did his rounds at night. On it was the date and time at which he called and the tickets were put in a little tin box in the porch. Several times a year – possibly once a quarter – they were collected by a policeman from another area, Minsterworth in our case. The local policeman accompanied him and they were usually invited into the kitchen and given a mug of cider. They both came on bicycles, of course.

The village shop was like Aladdin's cave and sold all sorts of things from groceries to buckets, brushes, brooms, boots and paraffin (not in the shop but in a shed at the back!). There was a bakery attached to the shop too and bread was delivered twice a week, as well as grocery orders. It was possible to go into the bakery itself to get bread hot from the oven and their dough cakes were the best I've ever tasted. Food was also supplied to tramps who were given vouchers to exchange for it – bread, cheese and tea were provided. The tramps were probably on their way from Westbury workhouse to either Ross or Ledbury. (Newent workhouse closed in 1915 and became the grammar school.) Tramps were allowed to sleep in a barn which belonged to the family who owned the shop.

There was a good butcher in the village who delivered over quite a wide area, though our meat came from the Longhope butcher, who also delivered and there was a fishman who called once a week. Travellers from various agricultural companies also came from time to time to see my father, and gypsies came round with pegs.

There was a blacksmith's shop in the village and I sometimes went with my father to watch the horse being shod, which was fascinating.

There was and still is a post office in the village, which also sold newspapers, cigarettes, sweets and some groceries. The post came out from Gloucester and was sorted here, then delivered by the village postman – and during and after the war by a postwoman. There were two deliveries a day for a very long time. There was a reading room, built in 1885 by the then rector for the men of the village. Daily papers were provided and also card games, draughts, chess etc. My father was the secretary of it for several years. It was pulled down about 20 years ago.'

NICKNAMES

'The use of a nickname was generally an indication of a person's popularity, although in some cases they could be slightly derogatory. In others they indicated the area or town from which a non-local originated. In all cases the true Gloucestershire dialect was used. I can recall many nicknames in common use at Dursley in the 1930s, some of which even by today's uninhibited standards would be unfit for publication!

All Welshmen were called "Taffy", all Scotsmen "Jock" and all Irishmen "Paddy". Those from the northeast were all "Geordies" and in other cases some were known by their town of origin, ie

"Brummie", "Cockney", "Bristol", "Oldham" etc. This also applied to those born much nearer to home. Stroud people were always called "Stroudies" and those from Chippenham "Chippies". Gloucester residents were called "Spotties", presumably after the Gloucester Old Spot pig! To have been born in the Forest of Dean, especially in Ruardean, would attract the nickname "Bear".

While most name calling was taken in good grace it was known that Foresters were very sensitive to the often repeated question, "Who killed the bear?" and it was not unknown for a fight to start between the persistent name caller and the exasperated Forester. However, this would soon be over and they would be the best of friends, "old butties" again as the Forester would describe it.

Moving nearer to Dursley, it was the people living in Nympsfield who were subject to most leg pulling and name calling. "Nympy", as it was always called, was then so isolated that its inhabitants were always considered to be a little bit eccentric to say the least. It was alleged that one local inhabitant put his pig on a wall to see a brass band pass by.

This little ditty was often repeated in jest when leg pulling was taking place –

"Nympy is a funny place
Stands up a tump
Everybody there eats
Ag pag dump."

To explain this, "ag pags" were sloes and "dump" was a pudding. It also explains why Nympsfield residents were known as "ag pags".

Those living in the parish of Coaley were always known as "Coaley Crows", and very often the younger element knowing that a particular Coaley resident would react, would approach that individual flapping their arms and calling out "caw, caw", only to be chased by the "crow" and be given a good slap if caught.'

PRANKS AND GHOSTS

'In 1906 there were two main political parties, Conservative and Liberal. The people of Sapperton were divided. Mrs Carrington worked for the Liberal cause and, by hanging out a yellow flag, made her views known. On this occasion, Mr Essex, the Liberal, was returned to Parliament. Mrs Carrington made much of this and teased known Conservatives when she saw them. Late one dark night they painted her door blue (the Conservative colour). To put people off the real culprits, they dribbled the paint to various houses including the police station and the rectory. The dog didn't bark and the family knew nothing of this until the morning. There was much talk and speculation as to who had done it. I remember asking my father if he had done the painting. He replied, "No, but I know who did!" Villages were not quiet little places where nothing happened; such incidents were talked about for weeks.'

'Gypsies visiting a local inn at Westbury on Severn one night created a drunken disturbance and were told not to come again. In their anger they laid a curse upon the inn. For a week afterwards showers of pebbles, large and small, descended onto the roof and churchyard, much to the alarm of the local people. Braver men formed a search party to try and find the cause. Some time later, the men found a huge catapult fixed up in a tree in nearby woods by means of which the gypsies had been bombarding the inn.'

'My great great grandfather on my father's side of the family, whose name was William Dyer, was a wheelwright for the mighty Crawshay family. The Crawshays owned extensive iron and coal interests in the Cinderford area. William Dyer and his family were the last people to have lived at the Old Grange at Littledean. The Old Grange is reputed to have been haunted and was an old mansion house. At that time it was owned by William Dyer's employers, the Crawshays.

William's daughter Emily, my great grandmother, had many a ghost story to tell about the Old Grange but none so strange as the one experienced by my great grandfather, Jimmy Morgan. Jim was courting Emily at the time, and it was when he was on his way back from seeing her that something very strange happened late one night.

Jim and Emily had said their goodnights at the gates of the Old Grange and Jim was on his way back up Lovers Lane towards Cinderford. Just in front of him a strange roaring wind seemed to cross the lane – whatever it was it scared poor Jim out of his wits, for he was to remember it for the rest of his days. On passing that part of the lane the next morning Jim could see that a large part of the hedgerow had been ripped right out for a considerable distance, not the sort of thing you would expect to happen on a quiet moonlit night.

Jim Morgan was a miner and had walked many miles through dark woods to and from work and was certainly not a man to scare easily. His words to Emily were, "Em, there's somethng very strange about this place." Jim and Emily Morgan spent their life in South Wales never to return to the Forest of Dean to live, but Jim never forgot the Old Grange at Littledean.'

THE GLORIOUS GLOSTERS

'Being a Gloucester city boy, I well remember those "Glorious Glosters" marching back to barracks at Robinswood on their return from Korea. Crowds lined the sides of Reservoir Road. With a mate, I used to scurry round the butts at the barracks scavenging for spent cases and bullet heads. I had the pleasure of meeting Colonel Carne VC when I was about 14 years of age. I wonder if he's looking down on us now as he did then – a towering figure in a bowler hat.

I also remember the day my father backed his Scammell tank up the road where we lived to show it off. He left a lamppost leaning at 45 degrees less than it should have been!'

THINGS I MISS

'Although I still live in a village I miss the smells and sounds of years ago. The clucking of chickens and occasional crowing of a cockerel in every other back garden; the happy sounds of children at school playtime; bean fields with their superb, heady scent; the singing of children at their games and men at their work; the clip-clop of working horses' hooves; the scent of primroses and cowslips we gathered from the fields for May Sunday at chapel; the scent of bonfires on a late autumn afternoon; newly sawn wood at the sawmills or Harry Vick's factory in South Street; freshly mown hay; moon daisies and dog roses; lilies of the valley under the parlour window in early June. All these and many more typify the Uley I knew and loved.'

CHURCH AND CHAPEL

At the heart of the community was the church or chapel, and many people can remember when Sunday was truly a day of rest, with regular attendance at church and Sunday school for the children a normal part of life. Sunday school also provided the children with what might be their only outing of the year.

SUNDAYS WERE SPECIAL

'Only the needful work was done on Sunday. Vegetables were often prepared the evening before for Sunday dinner. We went to the morning chapel service at Box, and after dinner went visiting uncles and aunts for tea, or we just went for a walk as a family. One of my Sunday memories is of walking through the village at about 8.30 on a summer evening with doors open and the sound of the *Sunday Half Hour* hymns coming from the radios. My mother often spoke of her younger days when a group of musicians would gather in a garden on summer evenings to the delight of villagers who leaned or sat on the

Longwell Green church members. The local church played a central part in our lives.

Getting ready for an outing from De la Bere at Southam in the early 1900s.

walls to listen in the still of the evening.'

'We always ate a Sunday lunch of roast meat (usually beef), fresh vegetables from the allotment, and rice pudding. Not so my grandmother and grandfather who reputedly deemed it "wicked" to cook on the Sabbath, so ate Saturday's leftovers, fried by my grandfather. My grandmother was taking no risks!'

Our Lives Revolved Around The Church

'I remember so much of our lives in the 1920s revolved around

the church. Ours was St Phillip's and St James', Leckhampton. Every Good Friday we went to church in the evening for a magic lantern slide show. It was a real highlight of our life; all the slides had a religious theme, but we thought it was wonderful. The church hall was used so much. The men, including my father, went to play billiards there several nights a week. Mother was in another room playing whist, and occasionally dancing. My sister and I loved to watch.

Then there were the concerts. I made my stage debut there at five years old, dancing as a golliwog, and my sister was a doll.

There were many poor families in the vicinity. Each autumn these families used to go to the church hall and hire blankets for the winter. They used to pay 6d for a blanket. They had to return it on a certain day in the spring, washed clean, ready for next autumn. One poor family was also provided with free heavy-duty lace-up boots. Girls and boys wore them. They looked awful and when we said so to Mother she said, "Just be glad you don't have to wear them".'

'Church played quite a large part in life at Stow on the Wold in the 1930s, although for our family it was a Non-Conformist circle where we attended the Baptist church. Sunday schools were well attended and the Anniversary was one of the high spots of the year. A new dress and hat were worn, with ankle strap patent leather shoes. The whole rostrum was taken up with tiers of children, and we were expected to sit there in full view of the congregation for two whole services, and sing the new hymns we had been rehearsing for weeks. On Good Fridays the North Cotswold Sunday School Union held a day of services at five churches – Moreton-in-Marsh, Cutsdean, Chipping Norton, Bourton and Stow, each taking a different year. Prizes were awarded to those who had won them for entering the Scripture Examination that year, and there was great excitement wondering which Sunday school had won the Shield.

A place which will be remembered by many Sunday schools in the area was the pleasure park at Bishop's Cleeve. The trip through unfamiliar country was an adventure, only surpassed by the large play area with entertainment for all ages from sand pits for the youngest to tennis courts for the older teenagers. For those in between there were swings, roundabouts and slides, with no limit on how many rides you had. I especially remember the largest slide – too high to be under cover. Mats were collected at the bottom, and taken up the high metal staircase. We had to be careful that the boys did not tread on our mats as we started down. This was a favourite trick, leaving unsuspecting girls to slide down on their knickers. At a certain time our Sunday school, one of several accommodated on that day, were called in for tea served at long tables. Then it was out again for more rides before spending the sixpence given to us on the bus. We were able to buy small gifts for 1d to 2d for the rest of the family, and a posy of flowers for Mum from buckets outside.'

SUNDAY SCHOOL AND THE RATCLIFFS

'Mrs Ratcliff came to the De la Bere at Southam as a middle aged widow in 1900 with her eight surviving children, four girls and four boys. She rented the De la Bere as well as land up to Queen Wood as part of the estate. Mrs Ratcliff was a wonderful woman who did a lot of good in the village.

One thing she did was to start a Sunday school for the village children and we went every Sunday afternoon, taught by Mrs Ratcliff or Miss Phyllis Ratcliff. The girls and boys had separate classes. At this time the house had no electricity but relied on oil lamps and log fires.

The Sunday school party was a great treat. At Easter the Ratcliffs would hide Easter eggs in the thick hedges that surrounded the big lawn and we would have to search for them. What excitement when we found one! There was also the summer outing. We would all get in the charabanc, including parents. Then we set off, usually to a place near a river, such as Evesham or Stratford. There we would go up the river in a boat, run races and have tea. Our parents would be given a more substantial meal. On the way back one of the Ratcliffs would come round with a large jar of sweets and distribute them.'

NEW CLOTHES

'We always had a new dress and a pair of sandals for Easter but were only allowed to wear them for Sunday school and had to change when we got home.'

GETTING ABOUT

Memories of the days before the motor car, when roads were quiet and dusty; of the first cars and the first country buses; and of steam trains, those friendly giants that were such a treasured part of our past.

THE DAYS BEFORE CARS

'There were very few cars in the "good old days" in Shipton Oliffe. Two carriers journeyed to Cheltenham every week and would do any necessary shopping for you that could not be obtained from the village shop. You were considered to be lucky if you had a bicycle, otherwise everyone walked to work. If you worked on a farm, you took your bread and cheese and cold tea in a flail, slung over your shoulder.'

'Mr Stanley owned a horse and waggonette in which he transported May Hillites to Gloucester on a Saturday shopping spree. It started off at 8.30 am from the Hill, arriving in Gloucester at midday and left for return at five o'clock, getting back to the Hill at 8.30 pm. He also acted as a carrier and would do errands, picking up medicines and other articles. By 1922 buses were introduced to the nearby A40 at Huntley. They had solid tyres and were very bumpy driving over roads surfaced only with broken stone. Pneumatic tyres appeared a few years later, on the front two wheels only; later, on the rear wheels also.

Most people used "Shanks's Pony" but some were lucky enough to have bikes, commonly called "bone shakers" which also had solid tyres. To make the tyres last longer, some men put studs into the solid rubber tyres. Later we were able to use the train from Longhope, which was reached through the many footpaths or the bus from Huntley.

The local policeman was strict and very keen. He was known to hide for some time behind a hedge to catch someone riding a bike without lights.'

'There were many horse-drawn vehicles during the 1920s, and

"Great Uncle Whale" outside his shop in Tewkesbury in the 1930s, with a real bone-shaker of a bicycle.

A popular mode of transport in the 1930s.

Mr Fluck, the carrier at Tibberton, was still very busy. There used to be signs at the bottom of people's gardens saying, "Mr Fluck to call".'

'Up to the 1930s the most common form of transport was the pony and trap. Children were brought to school in a horse-drawn vehicle and relatives in nearby villages were reached by pony and trap. Generally, families all lived fairly locally.

Bicycles were also popular and many people have memories of the district nurse cycling out to Leighterton from Doughton, with a basket on the front of her bicycle in which could be found sometimes a rabbit or pheasant. In the 1940s and 1950s motorbikes with sidecars were often seen in the lanes.'

'A motorbike owner offered his friend a lift from the Glasshouse on May Hill and was later horrified to find that he had lost his passenger. The friend had had enough early on and took the opportunity to slip off quietly as the driver slowed for a corner.

Shortly after the First World War a Mr and Mrs Davis, who ran a toy and fancy goods shop and Spirella Corset agency on the corner of Bull Lane in Gloucester, began a bus service through Taynton to Newent and Ledbury. The top of the bus was reached by ladder at the back and occasionally passengers found their way up there as well as parcels. Eggs being carried to Gloucester sometimes came to grief when the bus started suddenly and during flood times, passengers sat on the backs of the seats to keep their feet out of the water. But they always got through!'

WHEN THE ROADS WERE QUIET

'When we were young we trundled our iron-rimmed tricycles along the blue brick paths at Northleach, long since replaced by tarmac, and played safely on the main road, keeping just a wary eye open for the slow-moving cars of the day, which were driven in stately fashion through the town. The first child to spot a vehicle would warn his playmates by calling "Car!" and we would all obligingly jump up on the high pavement of the West End, waiting patiently for the soft-hooded, high-wheeled car to pass, sounding its hand-operated horn. Sometimes a steam engine, having taken on a fresh supply of water from the brook

The bitter winter of 1947 brought us together in adversity, and here at Wyck Rissington the working horses played their full part in getting about.

and deposited a heap of hot ashes on its bank, would snort its way past us, sparks flying from its funnel.'

ROUGH TRACK ROADS

'Children at May Hill had long distances to walk to school in all weathers on rough track roads. They often had to manoeuvre around woodsmen, especially in Newent Woods, who "tusked the timber" (pulled it out of the woods with chains). The roads were deeply rutted and thick with mud. No wellingtons in those days so all the children wore boots, which were lined up to dry in front of the fire at night. Boots were always mended at home, where fathers had a "foot iron". Sheets of leather were purchased and cut to size.'

TRAVELLING BY STEAM BOAT

'When I was young in the early 1900s I lived some twelve miles from Gloucester on the banks of the river Severn. Our only way to get into Gloucester, if you did not own a horse and trap, was by carrier's van or by steamboat, which ran a service from Gloucester to Sharpness along the canal. We lived in Framilode and would board the boat at Saul junction.

We younger people, when reaching our teens, preferred to travel by the steam boat. In summer it was lovely to sit on the deck of the *Wave* or *Lapwing* (as the two steamboats were called). The boats would start from Sharpness point about 8.30 to 9 am, reaching the junction with the Stroud canal just before ten o'clock. This was halfway to Gloucester. Another hour or so saw us in Gloucester docks.

The return journey was at 3.30 pm. It was a lovely journey, full of interest, and we always looked out for people we knew at any of the nine bridges and at the landing stages. It was so very peaceful and exciting – meeting the tugs coming down from the docks, waving to the sailors who were going with empty vessels to Sharpness and then on down the channel to Avonmouth – often calling out messages to relations.

It cost 10d from our landing stage on the top deck and 8d on the lower deck. No crowds, plenty of room to change your seat to talk to someone you knew. There were two cabins you could use and a toilet. The journey could still be quite pleasant even if it rained, or snowed. The only snag was that if you had a lot of shopping it was half a mile to walk to some of the villages from the landing stage, although some were quite near.'

THE GLOUCESTER AND BERKELEY CANAL

'The Gloucester and Berkeley Canal (now named the Gloucester and Sharpness Canal) was utilised very commercially during the 1930s. Large coasters, which only just got through the bridge openings, were regular visitors to Gloucester from Holland, Belgium and Denmark. Larger vessels bringing timber were unloaded at Sharpness on to smaller boats called lighters. These were pulled up the canal by tugs. I still love the smell of timber – you could smell it long before the boats reached the bridge near my home.

Behind the lighters there were always narrow boats carrying salt or coal. Whole families lived on these small boats, always smiling and happy. Donkeys on the footpath pulled the boats.

Unlike today, bridges were in two parts, one opened by the

bridgeman, the other by a passman who rode his bike from Gloucester to Sharpness (or vice versa) every day, or perhaps twice a day.'

THE FIRST CARS

'My grandfather was the first person to own a car in his village, the old Ford model with solid tyres. He never learned to drive it, preferring to ride round his farm in the late afternoon on his old cob with his dog at his heels.'

'Very few people at Arlingham had cars in the 1930s and those that did were mostly farmers, the doctor or the district nurse. If you heard a car in the night it meant either someone having a baby or being ill.'

'We lived at Slad vicarage in 1930. The first family car I can remember was a Trojan, a sort of tin soapbox on wheels. The

21ST., BIRTHDAY PARTY.

The Rev. & Mrs. Cheales

request the pleasure of your company

At a Party to celebrate the coming of age

of "Appa" (A.P.A. 657)

their faithful Austin Seven,

on Friday, January 2nd., 1952, 8p.m. till 10p.m.

Wyck Rissington Rectory,
Cheltenham.

R.S.V.P.

Early cars became members of the family – the Cheales' Austin Seven was 'born' in 1931.

back seat was a padded bench, easily removable and handy when my mother wanted to take her goats to visit Mr Billy! It had one drawback – it caught fire occasionally. The solution was to stop and hurl clods of earth at the engine, which was under the front seats.'

'The A48 is a dominant factor in the lives of people from Gloucester into Wales. Today it has been straightened and flattened, but in 1920 and for many years after it was a formidable highway. The early cars could not always get up its steep hills and after several attempts, would reverse and try going up backwards. At weekends and after school, some older boys, for pocket money, would stand near the steep places and push stones under the rear wheels to keep the car from running backwards while the driver paused to let the engine cool before trying again.'

The First Buses

'Chedworth was fortunate in having a railway and a bus service, making it quite easy in the 1930s to travel to town and beyond. Before the railway opened in 1890 the only way for a housewife to go to town for special shopping would be to beg a lift with the carrier. I remember my mother saying that her mother used to do this about once a year. The first bus service by Harveys used a large, solid tyred charabanc with a fold-back roof. In the week it would pick up passengers all through the village and could also be hired for outings, but on Thursdays the same vehicle would have its seats removed and be used to transport sheep to market.'

'My father used to drive the mail coach to Cirencester. My mother kept the horn he used for many years. He blew it at each village to collect the mail. Another of his jobs was to drive the commercial travellers to all the shops in a horse-drawn landau. The London coach used to stop at the Bull Hotel in Fairford to change the horses.

A Mr Norton started a bus service to Cirencester through Fairford when I was twelve in the early 1920s. Because it did not make much money he could not afford new tyres, so he put rope around the old ones.'

'There was a good bus service at Tarlton in the 1930s, from Bristol to Cirencester two or three times a day in each direction. We also had Mr Smith who drove his bus from Rodmarton through Tarlton and Coates to Cirencester every day; he also did errands and I remember seeing accumulators in the front being taken to town to be recharged for use in wireless sets.'

'The GWR ran a single decker bus service between Painswick and Stroud. It had two long seats facing each other with a narrow gangway. Sammy Adams was the driver. The conductor stood on the platform at the back and rang information to the driver – one ring meant stop, two rings start and three to say there was a vehicle behind wanting to overtake. The lamps used acetylene gas and so at lighting up time we stopped, the water was turned on to the carbide and when we were "lit up" we moved on.

By the driver were seats for two with the notice "These seats are reserved for smokers – ladies using them will be charged 3d extra". The discrimination annoyed me, so one morning I mounted the steps and took one of these seats in the front in the open air. The conductor looked embarrassed at his regular passenger's action and said he must charge the extra 3d. I paid, saying I was the equal of any man and where he could sit, so could I.'

The M&SWJ Railway

'The station at Chedworth was staffed until February 1956 when it was made an unstaffed halt and the stationmaster sent to Foss Cross. During the time it was staffed, small parcels and perishables were left here and often delivered by the station-master. For many years the daily papers arrived at the station on the train that arrived about 10.20 am and were then delivered around the village. For a time the *Echo* would arrive on the train from Cheltenham about 8 pm. Both lots of papers eventually arrived by road.

Milk traffic was sent to London from Chedworth until the mid 1930s. The heavier parcels and other goods traffic for the district were dealt with at Foss Cross which at that time seemed rather isolated, but also served a wider area. There was a coal depot here from which F. Harvey & Son and Bartletts of Ablington retailed coal all over the district, it being the principal fuel in those days. There was also a considerable traffic in agricultural products, hay and straw being regularly dispatched as well as grain and in the earlier years a good deal of horse traffic and other livestock, both in and out.

Usually the staff there consisted of a stationmaster, two signalmen, a porter and sometimes a lad porter. This gradually dwindled until in the final years the stationmaster and one signalman comprised the staff. Parcels traffic was distributed by a three times a week lorry service. Another service at Foss Cross was the holding and leasing out of corn sacks to local farmers to bag their grain. This was a service carried out by railways all over the country but of course has died out with bulk carrying.

Foss Cross had the lime works at its southern end, the railway bringing in coke and taking some of the lime traffic out. In earlier years stone was sent from Foss Cross to Tidworth to be used in the construction of roads at the army camps in that area. A lot of this stone was dug between Foss Cross and Fields Road Bridge where it can be seen that the cutting is very wide.

The line of rail itself was maintainted by the "gangs" as they were known. Each gang was composed of a ganger, a second man and about three lengthmen. There were two gangs based at Chedworth. One looked after the line Chedworth to Andoversford and the other Chedworth to Cirencester. Each gang was equipped with a motor-trolley and trailer whilst the ganger had a small motor trolley to himself as he usually rode his length each day, to see all was well. Once a week each length was walked by one man complete with hammer to ensure the keys holding the rails were not missing. In the summer, grass was mown along the fences and other places where it was liable to get set on fire with sparks from the engines, there being a danger of fire spreading to ripened corn fields.

The railway was probably in its heyday about the time of the Great War but in 1923 came the grouping of the railways and the M&SWJR was taken over by the GWR. A temporary resurgence came during World War Two but it never regained its former glory after nationalisation and then in June 1958 services were reduced to one passenger train each way per day and one freight from Swindon to Andoversford and return. The layout at Lansdown Junction, Cheltenham was altered and the M&SWJR train ran into Cheltenham St James station, thereby severing any direct route to the north.'

A Meeting Place

'For a small place like Grange Court the station seemed remarkably imposing, but it was a meeting place for several different companies. The Gloucester and Dean Forest line was formed under the auspices of the GWR in order to connect the Hereford and Monmouth line with Gloucester. Later the line was extended to connect with South Wales. Separate East and West signal boxes existed in the early days, situated near a road bridge. Signalmen's wages were paid through the window; the men used to take a short cut on to the road to visit the local inn. Constant use wore down the stones in the wall to such an extent that they had to be replaced. In 1935 a new signal box was situated further along the line. The station was closed in 1964 under the Beeching cuts and the buildings were demolished.'

Grange Court Junction, so typical of the local stations.

THE RAILWAY STRIKE

'During the First World War some of the railwaymen went on strike, thus affecting the GWR at Gloucester. One driver and fireman refused to take their train any further. An army officer on hearing this told the waiting passengers, which included several small schoolchildren, that he was capable of driving a train having had considerable experience in South Africa. Everyone eagerly clambered aboard, and true to his word off went the train, much to the astonishment of the folks left standing on the platform.

At the first level crossing the keeper refused to open the gates. The "temporary driver" said it was all right as he would open them. This he did by driving straight through the gates, scattering wood, nuts and bolts over a large area of the countryside.'

BARBER'S BRIDGE

'The Gloucester-Ledbury line was a 17 mile stretch of line which left the Gloucester-South Wales line at Over Junction and joined the Hereford-Worcester line at Ledbury Junction. The first station from Gloucester was Barber's Bridge, then followed Malswick Halt, Newent, Four Oaks halt, Dymock, Greenway halt and Ledbury Town halt – Ledbury station was of course on the Hereford-Worcester line.

Barber's Bridge station was equipped to cater for passenger traffic, parcels, goods, cattle, horses and poultry etc. It had a five ton crane for loading round timber, cattle pens, and a weighbridge for weighing the loads of road vehicles (but not, of course, rail vehicles). It also had a small goods shed.

The last passenger train over the bridge ran on Saturday, July 11th 1959. The last freight train, whose mission was to collect all the empty rail vehicles left in the branch line sidings, ran on Saturday, May 30th 1964.

I was the last and am probably now the only surviving stationmaster of those who worked on the Gloucester-Ledbury branch. When I came here it was just five years after the severe winter of 1947 and I remember Mr Wilce telling me that during the floods that followed the thaw that year some wooden railway sleepers, that had been stored in the yard, came floating down through the station.

Barbers Bridge Monument
Memorial near Newent to Welsh Royalists
killed 1643

Mr M. P. Price, MP, used to call at the station. We used to have consignments of wild duck eggs, also described as hatching eggs, for the Grove, Taynton and Mr Price seemed to take a special interest in these. A story circulating among local railwaymen in those days was that when the land was sold by the Price family for the construction of the railway the agreement between them and the railway company contained a clause to the effect that Barber's Bridge station should be kept open to serve the Price family and the services of the resident stationmaster be retained for as long as the Price family so desired and that the station could not be closed without that family's consent.

In those days when the branch lines were still very much in use and so many people used the trains to go to work, the drivers, firemen and guards would know most of the passengers travelling from the smaller stations. In general quite a friendly atmosphere existed between train crew, station staff and passengers and quite often a train would be held, for a brief period, if one of the regulars was a bit late arriving to catch it.

One little story which, perhaps, I should tell was repeated to me several times by Harold Wilce. Old Mr Ford, who was well versed in the customs of the country and an expert trapper, was out rabbiting one day with Mr Wilce and the station porter when the ferret got stuck with a rabbit in the burrow. Now, one way of getting the rabbit out was to cut a long blackberry briar, push it down the burrow and rotate it, the object being to get the briar caught in the rabbit's fur, pull the rabbit out, then the ferret would come out as well. The only snag was, while the porter was pushing the briar down one hole, Mr Ford had his ear to another hole listening for some possible movement of the rabbit and the briar came up that hole and hit him right in the ear. Mr Ford then stood up in a right old temper and what he said to the porter I'm afraid I cannot repeat.

Sometimes when a train would pull into the station the driver would call me over and tell me that the train had struck a pheasant and as soon as I could I would go along to the spot the driver had described and look around. I had many a nice bird that way.'

A Happy Memory

'Before reorganisation Cheltenham had three railway stations, including St James – the terminus of the famous *Cheltenham Flyer*. Malvern Road served the line to Stratford-upon-Avon, Honeybourne and the "Tiddley Dike". Malvern Road station staff jealously guarded their reputation, and there was a "waiting list" to be employed there.

For some four years I travelled daily on the 8.10 am train to Malvern Road. Most people sat in the same carriage and myself being occupied flinging a bicycle at a porter as I was late, the door was always open to receive me. Returning was more interesting, as the station was on the Birmingham to Cardiff route, especially so when Cheltenham Races were near, and when productions were changing at the Everyman Theatre. One fascinating visitor was Dame Margaret Rutherford. Word would be sent "down the line" and a reception committee of station staff would be organised. A truck, sometimes two, for her luggage would be organised plus someone to take the dog from her maid. The train would arrive, and so would Dame Margaret, in a flurry of necklaces and shawls, and that distinctive voice coming from a first-class window, "Porter!" She revelled in the attention and "tipped well". She was treated with courtesy as were all the passengers at that station.

Awash with flowerbeds in the summer, and with a coal fire in the waiting room in winter, Malvern Road is sadly no more but has left a happy memory of steam engine trains.'

HOUSE & HOME

THE WAY WE LIVED THEN

From small town houses to country cottages, life was hard for many families. We remember the hardships, but also the warmth of family life and the character of those old homes.

LIFE IN THE COUNTRY

'My parents lived at Woodlands from 1925 to 1930 or thereabouts. In actual fact, as we had no car (to survive there without a car is itself a tale of another generation!) and as Woodlands' only access was through seven gates, each one tied together with string from Batch Farm and my parents were in their late fifties, we actually occupied the cottage from April till October and spent the winter in London – a seasonal life which was little short of paradise for a teenager at boarding school. That valley was a place of remoteness and beauty which was, to us, unequalled, even if our way of living had to be pretty rough. We grew our own vegetables and we carried the necessities of life over the common from the village shop. Bread came by van from Walklett's – the delivery man parked in Haregrove Drive, walked down field and over the footbridge and up the orchard and probably climbed the six bar gate into the cattle pen to reach our never locked front door. Meat used at one time to come by post from Cheltenham, but I think Painswick acquired a butcher with a van; and a fishmonger, whose shop was in Gloucester Street, Painswick, used to call too, so did the oil man.

Woodlands at that time was unaltered, save that an outside bathroom had been added and linked to the house with a porch; I imagine now that it had always been the washhouse for at 6 am my father used to rise and put a light to the copper fire and come hell or high water, we all got our bath or hot shaving water as required by the simple method of dropping a hose into the copper and sucking at the other end before letting that end fall into the bath; it was rain water and gorgeous and I can still feel the sting of the smell of woodsmoke in it.

The cottage door furniture appeared to be complete – a door key near enough to a church key for size, was always "hidden" under the mat or in the eaves if we were out for the day; there was a good knocker and just inside the door it still kept its burglar proof bar – a three inch square oak post which pulled out of its socket and slipped into a tough iron hasp across the door. The kitchen and sitting room were floored with beautiful Guiting flags which took a surface polish like marble and the sitting room fireplace had a full equipment of pot hooks which we kept in use with a huge iron kettle, a very fine fireback and a bread oven with a handsome iron door with a classic figure moulded on it. Most of the windows were still leaded with the original loop-handle cleat fastenings and there was a little beauty up in the gable lighting the attic staircase across a two foot sill, from the which there was superb view of the shoulder of the common pushing up over Haregrove and Adderwood.

The village spring; that *was* in our day. The village water supply was a pretty mucky pond available to ducks, cows and horses, with a running spring and place for a bucket at one end; and in, I think, 1927, the spring became contaminated and diphtheria swept through the village where there were children and several died.'

'I remember visiting my grandparents in 1934. They lived in a thatched cottage in Dorsington, a hamlet, with no school or pub, then in Gloucestershire but since included in Warwickshire.

The cottage was very dark so the front door was left open all day. The floor seemed to be great curved pieces of stone and at the rear was a lean-to wooden building called the 'ovel' in which there was a copper used for the washing. Some of the window panes were of oiled paper and there was a round galvanised tin bowl with two handles on a rough wooden bench, in which to wash your hands after doing the gardening.

A village tap had just been installed at that time, which happened to be immediately over the road from their cottage, on the green, so we could easily walk over and fill a bucket of drinking water which was kept in the very cool pantry. Before that, the drinking water had to be fetched from a spring across the fields called Udd well, using two buckets hanging on a wooden yoke – kept in the ovel.

There were two large bedrooms with a door between them that was about three feet from the floor so you went up three wooden steps, through the door and down three more steps into

Cottages at Wyck Rissington were typical of those many of us grew up in.

the next bedroom. The wooden latch made a lovely sound as you shut the door. The mattresses had feather fillings in which you could sink down and wallow if you wished. On cold nights, a brick would be heated in the oven of the range, wrapped in old flannel and used as a foot-warmer in bed. Later, stone water bottles were used, along with oil lamps and candles for lighting.

Most men in the village worked on the land for the owners, cycling many miles, or walking, to get to work. If they got to work and it rained, they couldn't work and sat waiting in any convenient shed hoping it would stop because they got no pay that day as their rates were for piece-work. No money for the day was called 'Ovel bonus' as they sat it out in the ovel (shed).'

Town Houses

'I lived in Tewkesbury in the 1920s. Our family of six lived in a very small terraced cottage with three bedrooms, a kitchen and front room. There was no bathroom – the kitchen sink was the only place for running water in the house. There was a small backyard and the lavatory and coalhouse were off that. Cooking was done on a blackleaded range heated by a coal fire. Most houses in Tewkesbury at that time were small. There were only gas lights or paraffin lamps for lighting.'

'We slept three to a bed when I lived in Tewkesbury – lovely and warm. Life was what you made it and if you came from a large family there was always something going on, even if the money was scarce. The corner shop was the place for gossip – goods were bought on tick and paid for on pay day.'

THE FIRESIDE

'Cooking was done and water was heated on the open fire. The hearth rug was home-made from odd bits of material cut into strips, with a hessian backing. On Sunday afternoons or Bank Holidays it was replaced by a newer one. Our other downstairs room (the parlour) had a fire lit on Sunday in the winter, at Christmas and on special occasions.'

'Many families at Nailsworth in the 1920s lived in stone-built houses or small cottages. Nearly all had flagstone floors laid directly on the earth and exterior walls had no damp course. In winter these homes were difficult to keep warm and cosy. The floor was first covered with linoleum to hold the damp down. This was covered with coconut matting and over this was a good covering of home-made rugs. Rugs were made by threading strips of cloth through a strong sack with a special needle. All the family worked at it in the winter and all old clothing was used.'

CLEAN UPSTAIRS AND DOWN

'Every day of the week had its routine. Monday was washday and Tuesday for ironing. On Wednesday it was downstairs cleaning – things needed a once-a-week special clean as well as the day-to-day run through. Brass door knobs were to be polished, as well as all those china ornaments to be washed. Then there were the flues on the kitchen range needing cleaning and the soot from the throat of the chimney to be removed to stop it from catching fire.

The front or best room or parlour needed its clean, although it was only used on Sunday afternoons and evenings. I was allowed in to water the plants on the window sill and also to practise on the harmonium. I loved to go in with my grandmother while she practised the hymns for chapel on Sundays.

Upstairs cleaning was done on Thursday – the bedrooms usually had lino on the floors with bedside rugs, usually handmade, for the winter evenings. The lino came in handy when the bed ticks needed changing, as flock and feathers were spilt when the changes were made. It was a very tedious, dusty job opening the tick and carefully pouring the filling into the clean one before quickly sewing it up to stop further feathers escaping.

The dirty tick was taken into the garden or yard, turned inside out and the loose flock shaken free, usually over oneself. Then it was washed and dried and rubbed every inch all over with hand soap to make it feather proof.

Another aspect of bedroom cleaning was that, even if you lived beside the road, the bedroom windows were flung open wide and a rug would be vigorously shaken or dust-laden mops twirled, often over the heads of unsuspecting passers-by.

On Fridays, shopping meant a trip to Nailsworth. It was a time when you could leave an order and pay at the shops and they would deliver for you. There was still much to be carried however, and in those days short-cut footpaths went in all directions up Nailsworth hill, but, alas, they are all overgrown now. I well remember my grandmother in her seventies tracking up the hillside paths with baskets full of shopping.

Friday evenings would be the time set to cook a piece of bacon or boiling meat purchased while out shopping, filling the room with a wonderful aroma. But if Fridays had their "up" side, there was the "down" side too. It was syrup of figs night! Also bath night – oh, what fun! – or was it?

Saturdays, usually for me, after the syrup of figs, meant an early start. There was also a great deal of cooking to do; cake-making, pies and things in preparation for Sunday. Some Saturday afternoons we would catch the bus to Stroud for shopping for clothes or shoes, or for me to choose material from which my mother would make my clothes.

Some Saturday evenings after a hot day a stroll in the village was in order, stopping to chat to folk who were sitting on their garden walls, often shelling freshly picked peas and beans for their Sunday dinner. The older ladies would still have their aprons on and a ball of wool in their pockets attached to the socks they were knitting for their menfolk. Only the needful work was done on Sundays. Vegetables were often prepared the evening before. We went to the morning chapel service and, after dinner, went visiting uncles and aunts for tea, or we just went for a walk as a family.'

Keeping Time

'A good clock or watch was a must in the 1930s, as there was no church clock at Chedworth and often no radio. The trains kept very good time and many people would set their clocks by them, but at noon every day a bell would be rung at the vicarage for the benefit of those close enough to hear it.'

Water & Washday

Every drop of water was precious when it had to be fetched from the spring or the well — and, of course, no running water meant no indoor sanitation! Washday used many gallons of water, and was a weekly chore that did indeed last all day.

Fetching the Water

'In the late 1940s there was no public water supply at Duntisbourne Abbots. A few of the larger houses had wells, but the rest of us filled our buckets from the nearest pool or spring. One old inhabitant owned a yoke on which he hung two buckets and carried them 200 yards uphill, filled with river water.'

'Many people still living in Leighterton remember the village without running water. At the turn of the century there were over 20 wells in the village which supplied drinking water, but there was great concern over the need to improve the water supply. As recently as 1954 the West Gloucestershire Water Company finally implemented a scheme which had been under consideration for many years. Until then wells were shared between cottages and mostly these maintained good supplies except in cases of severe drought. Mrs Emily Frape recalls being able to kneel on the ground and scoop up water from the well and only rarely needed to let down a bucket on a rope.

A well was dug at The Slait in about 1927 and water was piped to Church Farm; several villagers were allowed to use the outside tap if their own supply was running low. A ram was used to pump water to different wells and into the fields for crop watering.

People recall having buckets strategically placed to collect rain water draining from roofs which was then used for washing. In Boxwell there was a stream which was used, up to 1954, for drinking water.'

'In the 1940s a quarter of the houses at Brockworth did not have a piped water supply. Many people shared a well and had to carry water at least 50 yards, and anything up to 200 yards for pure drinking water. Not only was the supply of water a problem, but so was disposal. In one instance, waste water ran down a bank to the end of the garden, over a footpath and then into a ditch. Ditches soon became clogged with soapy, greasy water and bits of food.'

'Living at Coopers Hill in the 1930s, we had several rain water tanks outside our bungalow but had to take buckets into my grandmother's bungalow next door to pump drinking water as there was no well on my parents' property. This meant going up and down seven stone steps with full buckets of water. Many a time I spilled water down my legs and into my shoes!

I can remember my mother washing up in a bowl with a metal tray on which to set the wet crockery. I used to earn sixpence a week if I did the washing up after tea. We did not even have a sink then but my mother had to fetch and carry water in buckets. Odd bits of soap were put into an enamel cup and hot water poured on to make a lather.'

'At May Hill water had to be got from a well, not our own but two doors away. The well had a bucket which was wound down several feet. You could always tell when it was full as it would jerk on the rope which held it. Up it came and we tipped the water into our own bucket and carried it back home. It was certainly a bit of a chore but the water was beautiful, clear and cool.'

'In the early part of the century at Kingswood Abbey young boys of 12 or 13 were often sent with a bottle or jug to fetch some beer for their father's supper. Several have told me that they used to take a good swig and then fill the bottle or jug to the proper level from the standpipe and take it home where Father was waiting. I never heard that anyone was caught.'

BATHNIGHT

'Baths were taken once a week in a tin bath in front of the fire, the water being heated in kettles, children first and when they were in bed, the parents followed.

At Nailsworth, if the head of the household was a miner a coal allowance was given as he needed a daily bath as well as the means of drying his clothes every day. He paid a reduced rate for this coal and arranged for its delivery to his home, usually by horse and cart.'

'We came to Slad vicarage in 1930 and while there I went to stay at Uplands with the widow of the previous vicar. It was there I had my experience of a genuine hip bath. There was a bathroom in the house but I was assured this was for the maid's use! The hip bath was duly hauled up the stairs and put on a mat in front of the gas fire and filled from jugs of water. The only trouble was that I am very tall and never did discover what one was supposed to do with one's legs.'

THE LITTLE HOUSE

'Before septic tanks were used in the 1920s, a local resident at May Hill undertook to knock on doors to ask if he was required to empty and bury their privy contents. It was his job also to walk to Huntley school once a week to deal with the school loos.'

'When I was a child about 70 years ago I used to visit relatives in the Brimscombe valley. Their house was on the side of a stream. To visit the toilet you had to go to the top of the house to a small, square room. Here was a board with two round holes cut out, one slightly smaller than the other. Through them you could look straight down into the stream. It was always very frightening to me.'

'Toilet rolls were unheard of in the early 1930s. We diligently cut up papers into squares and when we had got a fair sized bundle, threaded string through a hole made in the corner with a metal meat skewer to form a loop. It was then ready to hang in the outside toilet for use. At Christmas, however, what luxury. We carefully smoothed out the tissue wrappers from the oranges, bought as a treat for Christmas, and used these instead. I must say though, that though they were softer and had a better, if strange, odour, they were not so interesting as the half snippets of news we read on the newspaper squares.'

'My early childhood was spent, in the 1920s, in a large Victorian house at Ebley. The house had been built for a prosperous local family but by this time it had been divided up for use by three separate families. The upstairs apartment had a touch of luxury in the shape of a flush toilet. This facility must have been very special for the servants who lived in that part of the house in their day. We were so impressed we almost took visitors to view it! There was a full width wooden seat which contained a deep pan and a recessed ivory handle which was raised to operate the flush. A lid could be closed down to obscure the whole from view. One word springs to mind — elegance!'

THE LOST TEETH

'In Painswick 60 years ago, what is now called Spire House was the butcher's shop next door to the Falcon where three generations of Tidmarshes had plied their trade. Behind it was the slaughterhouse and the yard where the cattle were held prior to slaughter.

People are apt to forget that between the period when the earth closet reigned supreme in rural areas and the advent of the modern flushing lavatory there was a sort of sanitary interregnum when we reverted to something much akin to the arrangements used by the Romans. What one had was a pedestal which gave directly onto a sewer without benefit of any bend in the pipe. This contraption was located at the top of the yard.

Now, Granny Tidmarsh was a lovely person but she did enjoy a bottle of stout and it was quite a lot stronger than it is today. Thus it came to pass that one day Granny Tidmarsh was sitting on the contraption at the top of the yard when she was seized by a most violent spasm of coughing in consequence of which her dentures went down the pan!

Some of the sewers in Painswick are pretty steep. The one in question went down the hill, down Stamages Lane all the way to the bottom to where The Little Bridge House now stands, for there stood the Painswick sewage farm presided over by one Danny Gardiner.

Of course Painswick was far from being affluent in those days and there was certainly no National Health Service, so apart from anything else the loss of a set of false gobblers was a major financial disaster.

So they ran, Eddy first, then Flora, Gran bringing up the rear, down past the Mary Home, on down past Pear Tree Cottage. Someone shouts, "What's up, Ed?" "Got to see Danny Gardiner, Gran's lost her teeth." On past the Cross Hands, and there at the bottom stood Danny, leaning on his rake like a semi-redundant croupier presiding over the infernal regions.

"Dan," they called, "have you seen our Gran's teeth?"

"No," replied Danny, "they b'aint a come down yet."

But then he called, "Oh, 'ere they be a coming now!" and he ups with his rake and scoops them out! One hopes that they rinsed them off in the stream, and all returned home with much rejoicing.'

WASHDAY

'At Rockhampton my husband, as a child, with his brothers used to take an old pram chassis on which was fitted an old galvanised bath, to collect water for their mother's washing from a brook some way off. Going was great as it was downhill, but coming back with the water, uphill, was not so good and woe betide them if the bath was only half full. They'd have a clip on the ear and have to go back again!'

'There was always great activity on Sunday evenings at Shipton Oliffe after church or chapel, when people were filling the copper for washday on Monday.'

'During school holidays in the early 1950s I would spend a lot of time at Stroud with my Grandma and Grandpa. One of my vivid memories was Grandma's washday which was every Monday without fail. They lived in a cottage, no running water, but with a well in the garden from which the water came. The washhouse was attached to the cottage and in the corner was the earthenware boiler which would be boiling non-stop every Monday.

My Grandpa's job every Sunday was to fill the boiler with water, lay sticks and paper underneath and leave sufficient fuel for the day's wash. First thing Monday morning before leaving for work he would light the sticks and put the first lot of fuel under the boiler. The water was then boiling when Grandma had finished her breakfast. Firstly the "whites" would go into the boiler together with the powder, I think it was Persil, and this would carry on boiling while she made sure that there was sufficient water in the tin baths on the old wooden bench ready for rinsing the whites. She would use a wooden stick, like a short broom handle to transfer the washing from the boiler to the tin bath. Next to the tin bath would be a blue bag on a long piece of string and a block of carbolic soap. The blue bag would be dipped into the bath for the whites and the carbolic soap would be used, if needed, on the coloured washing.

After the rinsing process it was the turn of the mangle. A bucket was positioned under the mangle to catch all the water, and if I was lucky I would turn the handle of the mangle. From there the washing went into a woven basket ready for hanging on the washing line. The washing line stretched all around the garden and props were placed near each pole. These props had been selected and cut down from the local wood by my Grandpa who had to walk through the wood daily to his place of work. He worked as a gardener at a big house. Washday did last all day and it took place every Monday whatever happened.'

'It was imperative at Uley to have one's washing on the line early on a Monday morning – a kind of status symbol. My mother's whites, after going through the rollers of the enormous mangle, were on the line before 7.30 am.'

'We were always told, "It's a poor Sunday that can't keep Monday", which meant cold meat and bubble and squeak – leftovers from Sunday dinner – for Monday lunch.'

FOOD AND SHOPPING

Home-cured bacon and hams, home-made wines and cider, elvers in season, good nourishing food cooked on the blackleaded stove – memories of a time when tradesmen delivered to the door and shopping was a pleasure.

GLOUCESTERSHIRE KINDNESS

'Most gardens at Box in the 1920s were packed with vegetables, fruit trees and herbs, for herbal remedies were necessary as doctors needed paying. Many gardens had a run for a few hens scratching around and fed on household scraps or garden waste. I just remember an old lady who kept a pig. Whether male or female, a long line of occupants of her sty were called "Charlie", and before the old lady had her breakfast every day both "Charlie" and the sty were scrubbed.

Bartering and giving or selling surplus fruit and vegetables was the order of the day. So many times, my mother used to say: "It's only Gloucestershire kindness to give away what you don't want." She meant it in the nicest way; not the cynical way in which it might be taken. It was my job on Saturday mornings to call at several houses to get kitchen scraps and, when in season, the very tiny potatoes that were too small to use. We boiled them up for our hens. When we had a glut of eggs, I would take some with me as a "thank you".

These days deep freezers contain things we used to bottle and larders were stacked with rows of kilner jars. Also runner beans were salted when in season and kept for months. Clamps were made in the gardens to keep vegetables in good condition. Preserving eggs, however, was a very careful job. You needed a large container or bucket and a tin of waterglass which was dissolved in boiling water, then allowed to go cold. Eggs with perfect shells were selected and duly placed in the solution, making sure they were covered and did not float. They could be kept for months in this way but when using them it was wise to break them before use.'

WHAT GOOD MEALS

'I can see the old blackleaded grates and ovens now. And what good meals were cooked in them! My granny at Chipping Campden used to crochet little nets from string and into these would go potatoes, in another went the greens and yet another would hold a bacon "jack" (a suet crust with bits of bacon inside) – all wrapped in a cloth and boiled together in a big black pot which hung over the fire. Another day, the Dutch oven would be set in front of the fire and perhaps a rabbit or a joint of meat would be cooked in it. The rabbit made a lovely meal – it cost about a shilling and you received threepence back for the skin.

Feeding the free range poultry in 1930.

When roasted or stewed and baked in a pie, it became a good or cheap meal. In the oven at the side of the fireplace, there was often a basin full of butter beans, covered with water and with a nice lump of dripping on top. A rice pudding would be left to cook overnight, ready for dinner the next day.

My mother being a very good cook, a talent inherited from my grandmother, traditionally began Christmas Day with breakfast consisting of home-cured ham and backbone pie (this was the backbone of the pig cooked then baked in a pie and eaten cold – delicious). My daughter and I continue this tradition, but alas with a pork pie – a poor substitute.

The fire was always kept going in the grate and was banked up at night with cinders and tea leaves saved from the tea pot. It was only allowed to go out when the clinkers were removed – this was the ash that dropped through the bars and was riddled for the cinders.'

'Beastings were regarded as a delicious treat. Sugar was sprinkled on to a pan of the first milk after the cow had calved. It was baked in a slow oven. When cooked it look like a rich egg custard and was known as cherry curds.'

The Best Wine and Cider

'Wine making was very popular in Shipton Oliffe, with great rivalry over who could make the best and strongest wine. No such things as demi-johns, the wine was made in a big crock pan and when you opened the door of the house, there was a strong smell of fermenting yeast. When it was completed it was then put into wooden barrels, ready to hand out to all who called for a drink.

One lady who lived on a smallholding kept ducks and chickens which wandered around the yard. This particular lady was famous for her home-made wines (or so she thought) and her young sons were very keen on going into the sheds and tasting the various liquids from the barrels. One morning the lady heard such a noise from the yard, the ducks were quacking in a frightening way and she thought "a fox". Out she went but the ducks were making such a noise, picking up their feet into the air as if to do the "goose-step" and then falling backwards on their rear. She was puzzled and eventually followed them into the shed and there was the offender, the dripping tap; one of the sons had not turned it off properly and the ducks were thoroughly enjoying this nectar. The next morning the yard was strangely silent, the birds sleeping – I wonder if ducks suffer from hangover?'

'Many families at Southfield made cider and home-made wines out of dandelions, cowslips, elderflowers, blackberries, damsons and parsnips.'

'Taynton Cider and Taynton Squash Perry were thought to be as good as champagne. Mr Gaymer of the Gaymers Cider Company bought his apples here as he considered them the best.'

ELVERS

'During February, March and April, elvers have always been esteemed as a delicacy in Gloucester and the bordering tidal reaches of the lower Severn. Elvers are the fry of the European eel.

I can remember when my mother used to buy them for 6d for a pint pot. She used to clean them at the pump with lashings of water then dry them off in a clean tea-towel. Sometimes my mother beat up an egg and stirred this into the elvers as they were cooking. As the season drew on the elvers developed a black line and then my father would not eat them. People came through the villages selling the elvers – one old lady conveyed them in a pram.

In 1943 the Epney Depot for collecting elvers was taken over by the Ministry of Agriculture and Fisheries and in 1948 when a London firm took over the Depot to export live elvers to Holland, the price of elvers soared and people could not afford to buy them, so the habit of elver-eating dropped considerably.'

'In the elver season the men used to come round Maisemore with their buckets full of elvers and sell them (or give them away if there was a glut). They used to be sold in Gloucester from tin baths and to indicate they were available a tea towel was put over the back of a dining chair outside the front door. I can remember my great aunt making elver pie in the 1950s. It was made of shortcrust pastry and the filling contained bacon, eggs, herbs, onions and, of course, elvers. It could be eaten hot or cold in slices.'

'In 1950 I was working as the district nurse at Arlingham, before the days when a bathroom in the house was normal. The standard equipment for bathing a baby was a jug and basin. One morning I went to a house and could not find the basin – it was full of elvers! The husband had been elvering and went round the village selling them at sixpence a pound, using all available buckets, bowls and zinc baths.'

KILLING THE PIG

'Of all the sounds of my childhood in the 1930s at Westbury on Severn the most haunting and most clearly remembered is the squealing in sheer terror of the family pig, prior to and during its killing. When I was young my grandmother would close the back door to the yard and play records on the old gramophone to shut out the frightening sounds.

On the appointed day the "butcher" (and indeed the local pig killers were often known by that name) would arrive usually accompanied by three helpers. They would rope the pig and eventually land it on its side on a pig bench, a long structure on four legs some nine to twelve inches high. Then, while the helpers held the hapless pig, the butcher's knife would strike home through the neck. Next came the burning off of the hairs, for which piles of dried fern had been gathered from the forest, and the smell tended to permeate the house.

In those far off days before refrigeration, the sides of bacon were salted and hung, supported by hooks in the ceiling, in a cool place. And in this way they served many breakfasts to come.

One usual effect after a pig killing was for the men to develop a rash of boils from the rich living, a complaint which is rarely heard of today.'

'Nothing was wasted when the pig was killed. The bladder was used as a football by the boys.'

'During the war we kept a pig to supplement the rations. When winter came a message would be sent to Mr Ford at Chedworth to come and kill the pig. He would walk over with a woven straw bag on his shoulder which contained his knives. Cold weather was a blessing during this period because we didn't have electricity to refrigerate anything. The hams were used at Easter or any other celebration that might occur. My mother always gave joints of meat to various people in the village and they would return the favour when their pig was killed.'

'We used "everything but the squeak", so when the carcase was opened up Mother set to at once, to preserve all the parts. The fat was placed in a huge iron saucepan on the range, to cook slowly all day, frequently stirred by anyone passing by. As the liquid fat appeared, it was poured into the bladder, which when full was tied up and placed on one of the hooks in the kitchen ceiling – the rich, white fat was used for Mother's excellent pastry. The "scrimpets" left after the boiling were a delicious extra.

The baked faggots were always a great favourite in our family; they were made from the liver, onion, breadcrumbs, pepper and salt and herbs, mostly parsley and sage. This mixture had to be put through the hand mincer, attached to the scrubbed kitchen table by a screw – which always seemed to come undone. I was usually asked to turn the handle whilst Elsie, our maid, pushed the meat into the mincer. Mother, in the meantime, was preparing the caul, a skin with fatty veins running through it. It had to be soaked in hot water to be soft enough to cover the faggots, which Mother formed in her hands after the mixture had been well stirred in a huge bowl. The faggots, placed in a large tin, were cooked in the bread oven next day, after the bread came out.

The chitterlings – or pig's guts – were soaked in big pans, in the washhouse; next day they had to be turned inside out through freezing running water. When Father was satisfied they were 100 per cent clean, they had to be plaited, my favourite job, but tricky; if I let go, they slipped undone in a trice. The pig's head was used to make delicious brawn, together with an old hen; apart from pepper and salt, nutmeg was always used.

The sides of bacon were placed in huge lead pans in the dairy. Mother had to rub them each day with a mixture containing saltpetre. Her poor hands suffered terribly, especially if she had a sore on them. After three weeks the sides of bacon and the hams were also hung on hooks in the kitchen.'

The Fairford butcher's cart in 1934.

Progress saw the demise of the deliveryman's horse and cart, and by the end of 1934, Fairford's butcher was using a van.

Callers to the Door

'In the 1920s milk was delivered to the door in Charlton Kings by a horse-drawn float with large churns on board. The milkman stood on a step at the back with the reins in his hand, but the horse knew exactly where to go and would walk along the road stopping at the appropriate customers' houses. The milkman came to the door carrying a metal milk bucket with metal measuring containers, or dippers, hanging on it. He then ladled milk out in pints or half pints, into your large china jugs. In some places they were not too particular about clean hands and a dirty thumb sometimes came into contact with the milk being poured into your jug.'

'I was about nine when I helped deliver milk with the local farmer at Brimscombe, Mr Wilkins ("Wilky"). I would go to his farm each morning in the school holidays and watch the cows being milked by hand, the milk being cooled and put into churns. Then Wilky would hook two churns onto the yoke across his shoulders, I would take a couple of one or two pint cans and we would go to the local houses. Wilky ladled the milk into the cans and I took them to the housewives, who poured the milk into their jugs. Some days he would carry apples in his pocket and give them to the kids in our street.'

'At Coopers Hill in the 1930s we used to have a visit from the grocer, who had a shop in Gloucester. Once a fortnight my mother gave him an order for the essential commodities like butter, sugar, tea etc, and he would deliver. Mother had a metal safe in which she kept all the "tender" things. This was situated in a cool place out in the garden under a hedge – the coolest place there was. There is still set in the ground a square cemented hole in which butter, margarine, sausages and meat were kept in pottery containers.'

'At Blaisdon in the 1930s bread was delivered by at least two bakers who came round with their horses and covered waggons. Two or three butchers called twice a week and the local grocer came round on Tuesdays and delivered on Fridays. He was a very helpful man, always asking, "Do you need anything else? Salt, pepper, vinegar, mustard, soap, soda, blue?" One local

By 1938, the Fairford butcher had yet another delivery van in use.

farmer had a milk round in the village and the fish man put in an appearance when it suited him.'

'Gypsies were constantly calling at May Hill with items, usually pegs, for sale. The true Romanies were thought of quite kindly but the diddicoys arrived on the scene and cashed in on the gypsy trade. They used to park at the side of the lane in Newent Woods from where they took dogwood to make pegs, binding the prongs together with narrow metal strips cut from cocoa tins and fixed with a spring. They worked until moved on by the local copper. They arrived on the doorstep with a basket of pegs which were sold for twopence a dozen. They were fulsome with their thanks and endowed you with good luck for the coming year if you bought from them, but it was a different tale if you did not – a few home truths or a curse were your lot!'

'The village of Upton St Leonards, then a small village just three miles from the city of Gloucester, was well served.

Stan, from Painswick Bakery, brought the bread to the back door in a huge basket, a couple of times a week. Bill Gardner, owner of a small shop in Chequers Road at the top of Barton Street, delivered the newspapers and the comics, and Mr Orpin from Alvin Street humped bags of coal from his lorry at the front gate to the coal house at the back of the house.

Friday morning was shopping time and Mum and I regularly visited Southern Stores on Gloucester Cross. Tins and packets lined the shelves and there was always action at the cheese counter. My mother stood one side of the counter and listed the grocery items she required while Tom Southern stood the other side of the counter, writing it all down. The goods were then all duly boxed up and delivered the following Monday by Lionel.

I nearly forgot – the Corona lorry came on Thursday afternoons!'

THE CO-OP

'I was born in 1946 and from my early childhood I can remember what an important role the Co-operative Society played in our daily lives.

Day-to-day purchases were made from one of the three grocery shops in our village of Ebley, near Stroud. However, the main order was placed at the Co-operative Stores in Cainscross about half a mile away.

Once a week my sister and I would walk to the Co-operative Stores with our mother. This establishment had a large grocery hall, bakery, butcher's shop, drapery department, furniture and hardware stores. The main building housed the grocery department.

When we walked through the doors we were confronted with a long, mahogany counter. We would take our place in the queue and wait until it was our turn to be served. This was no hardship in those days as there was always someone there that we knew and the time waiting was usefully employed exchanging news and gossip. When we reached the front of the queue an assistant was waiting to fetch our order, either from off the shelves behind the counter or from the warehouse beyond.

At this stage it was most important to give in your Co-op number because this would ensure you received the correct dividend at the end of the year. Alternatively an order book could be handed over to the assistant and the groceries delivered to your doorstep later.

Bread and cakes could be purchased at another counter in the grocery hall. Usually we visited this counter only to settle the account as bread was delivered on a daily rota by the Co-op breadman.

We then moved on to the butchery where meat hanging from hooks and displayed on marble slabs could be selected and cut by the butcher to the quantity required. This was wrapped in white paper and the butcher's lady assistant took the money. Meat could also be ordered and delivered on the day required. This service was useful as very few people had refrigerators or freezers in those days.

Sometimes Mother would buy something from the furniture department. There she would be advised by Mr Blick what was the most suitable and best quality for money. If Mr Blick said something was unsuitable then it wasn't purchased.

Occasionally, when our shopping was completed, as a special treat we would cross the road and have a cup of tea and slice of cake at the Co-op cafe across the road.

In those days the staff rarely changed and customer service was very important. On Coronation Day 1953 I can remember walking along to the Co-op Stores to watch the ceremony on a television set up by the Co-op for its customers.'

'The centre of Cinderford was undoubtedly the Co-op. Not just one but three, all in the High Street. The co-operative style of trading appealed to the thrifty locals for, once a quarter, a meeting was held and the dividend declared. I remember when it could be as much as half a crown in the pound returned to the members. "Divi day" was looked forward to for weeks. It meant new shoes for the children and a few little extras for everybody.

Best of all, our Co-op had a Penny Bank. It was for members' children and one could literally pay in one's carefully hoarded savings at a penny a time. But the real joy of belonging was that every summer there was a treat. In our Sunday best clothes we paraded through the town, enamel mug carried around our neck on a piece of white tape (courtesy of the drapery). The officials headed the procession with the town brass band playing rousing marches to buoy up our flagging spirits and weary legs on the long march to the slaughterhouse field. Here we were regaled with a bag of sticky buns, bread and butter, slab cake and biscuits, washed down with a cup of sweet milky tea from the huge urns. There were races and games, scrambling for nuts and those little biscuits with a sugar rosette on top. We sang and recited on the makeshift stage for a sixpence prize and went home tired and replete at about five o'clock. No wonder we looked forward all year to the Penny Bank Tea.'

PAYING THE BOOKS IN CHELTENHAM

'In my youth credit cards had not been thought of, but shops provided their trusted customers with "books" in which their purchases were recorded. Our family had books with the butcher, grocer, baker and milkman, and these were paid weekly.

Cook collected and checked the books and brought them to my mother who, after consultation with her, forecast next week's needs. This was summarised and presented to my father who wrote out a cheque.

Then my mother got out her cherished Royal Enfield bicycle (with a large basket behind the saddle) and set forth to "pay the books". First stop the bank to cash the cheque, then to the shops, starting with the grocer in Winchcombe Street. We never seemed to have to queue but were offered chairs on which to sit. After paying the necessary cash, next week's order was dictated. If cheese was on the list a sample was proffered on the end of a knife. Sometimes in the holidays I accompanied my mother, then I was offered a sample too.

So, on to the other shops except the milkman. Bottled milk had not been thought of and our requirements were ladled out into our own big jugs. Occasionally "Milky" gave us a ride in his float in which one had to hold on tight.

Other orders were always delivered, most shops had their own errand boys but there was a uniformed Boys' Brigade in Cheltenham. Most errand boys were unpaid by the customer but never failed to present themselves on Boxing Day. They always whistled, that's how we learned the popular tunes of the day, but nobody ever whistles now.'

Our Village Shop

'My home in the late 1920s was on a rather isolated farm. We walked to the village and the school, a distance of some one and a half miles.

On our way to or from school we passed the bottom of Post Office Lane, where our shop was situated. On the days when I had a penny or perhaps two halfpennies, as soon as school was over I would run and skip up Post Office Lane to Miss Midwinter's shop, eager to part with my precious coins.

Miss Midwinter was a rather big, voluminous lady, who never hurried regardless of how many customers were waiting to be attended, whether on post office or shop matters.

It was a traditional Cotswold stone cottage. The door opened directly into the shop – a room not big, partly divided by a wooden counter on which was a large pair of weighing scales with a flat white marble plate and numerous brass bell weights. Behind this was a stone slab containing large lumps of cheese, butter and lard, knives and wire cutters.

At the other end of the counter, in a small space, was the post office with its variety of ink pads, endorsing stamps, nib pens, ink bottles, blotting paper and forms of various descriptions.

A real treat for me was when occasionally my father would say on a Saturday night that he and I would walk to the village shop (which was always open on a Saturday until about 9 pm, or until the last customer was served), to get the groceries.

Dad and I would wait in the shop to be served, Miss Midwinter unhurriedly dealing with each customer in turn; perhaps taking down a side of bacon from its hook on the wall and carefully cutting the rashers, weighing and packing them. Waiting customers would sit on the bench seat alongside the wall exchanging village gossip, the men puffing on their pipes discussing the farm crops, animals, etc. I would be eyeing up the display of sweets and chocolate, knowing Dad would buy me and my young brother our Saturday night treat of a twopenny bar of Cadbury's chocolate, before walking back home laden with our purchases.

Miss Midwinter lived in the cottage with her unmarried brother Bert, who was the village carrier. Twice a week he would set off from the village with his horse and four-wheeled waggon to go to Cheltenham, some nine miles. He would buy any sort of goods villagers required, collect shop orders, deliver any type of parcel or visit the chemist for one's pills and potions.'

FROM THE CRADLE TO THE GRAVE

It was far more likely that we would be born, suffer illness and die in our own homes in the past, in the days before the National Health Service when home cures were passed down through families and the doctor had to be paid when he came to call. Many people also recall the scourges of childhood – the deadly infectious diseases such as scarlet fever that meant a long stay away from home and family.

HOME CURES

'When I was a child in the days before antibiotics, our cuts, grazes, boils or any sore places were always treated by my grandmother's marshmallow ointment. She made it by cooking marshmallow leaves and pure lard together. This was poured into pots and left to set, when the colour faded from green to almost white. It worked slowly but always seemed to clear up the various ailments. It had a very soothing effect whilst healing.'

'My Grandad was a do-it-yourself physician. If you had an ache or a pain anywhere he would have a "cure" for it. A true Gloucestershire son of the soil he diligently collected various plants around the farm and carried them back to the house to be hung from the kitchen beams in spidery bunches until, sere and crackling, they could be transferred to paper bags and stored in the dairy. The efficacy of his potions could be judged by the fact that he lived well into his nineties and had only once ever had occasion to call in the doctor – and that was to treat a dislocated shoulder he sustained in an altercation with his bull.

So it was quite natural for us to be treated with various concoctions as we passed through all the stages of childish ailments. Chesty coughs would produce his "aggermoney tea" (agrimony). Or perhaps as an alternative it would be coltsfoot leaves – dried and infused, this was for "wheezy" chests. Nettle stings were frequent and were soothed by the application of a bruised dock leaf; if it was a bee sting, a trip out to the pigsty was called for, to collect a couple of leaves off the houseleeks which grew in profusion on its pantiled roof. The juice of these leaves was also invaluable for styes (on the eyelids) and burns and scalds. Grandad dealt with warts by rubbing them with raw meat and burying the meat. As it rotted the warts disappeared. It was akin to magic – but you must never tell where the meat was buried or the cure would not work!

Abdomens came in for a great deal of attention. Lemon balm tea for stomach cramps, penny royal ditto for the wind. Both grandparents were "martyrs to the wind". Parsley, dried or fresh, was good for your kidneys and dandelion leaves in the spring (chopped and put into a sandwich) cleared the blood. Fragrant rosemary was a more pleasant remedy, in tea if you had a headache or, more popular with Grandma, as an infusion into the rainwater she used to wash our hair.

Luckily we didn't suffer with corns or we would have been running around with our socks full of ivy leaves. Grandad was also partial to the tiny, bright yellow-flowered tormentil which flourished along the paths around the farm. Known to him as "tarment" he used it, fresh or dried, as an infusion in which he bathed his feet. What with his bunions, hammer toes and corns this did not seem to be one of his most successful remedies. However, he did have his own pet cure for cuts and grazes. He would go into the barn or cowshed and wrap them in the fluffy cobweb from the rafters. I never knew him to get blood poisoning.

Like most children we had frequent bouts of earache. This called for the boiling of an onion until soft, taking out the central "pip" and inserting it – still hot – into the offending ear. Grating the horseradish for the Sunday beef was also guaranteed to clear a stuffy cold. But boiled horseradish was also used for worms – which must have been a common complaint in those days of insanitary cottages.

Poor circulation too, often led to chilblains and the sovereign remedy for these on hands or feet was by immersion in the contents of the chamber-pot. Perhaps it was the ammonia?

"Have you been?" The question which dominated our childhood. All our family seemed to be obsessed with bowels and the regularity thereof. Every Friday night was syrup of figs night, whether you needed it or not! Senna pods were stewed in water and then prunes were added. When soft, the prunes (and juice) were eaten. Talk about adding insult to injury! And as soon as the swallows returned in the spring we got dosed with brimstone and treacle. This was actually quite pleasant to take (but it did dire things to you when it reached the other end), however, down it had to go to "clear your blood". Blackcurrant tea was a much more palatable remedy for winter's coughs and colds – hence today's Ribena. Croup and whooping cough were treated in Cinderford by taking the young patient to the gasworks at the bottom of the town, to breathe in the fumes. Likewise, we were usually shepherded outside when the tar pot came along to mend the roads – another good remedy for weak chests.

I have left until last the queen of all Forest remedies – "ellum-blow tea" (it rhymes with "bough"). The pungent flowers were gathered in the spring, dried in the sun and stored in paper bags. One had only to sneeze in the winter and out would come the dreaded paper bag; a good handful was put in a jug, boiling water poured over, and covered with a teatowel and left to infuse. This evil-smelling brew had to be drunk willy-nilly. To this day I can recall that smell of tomcats which emanated from it – even the proverbial "spoonful of sugar" failed to make this medicine go down without protest. Feverish colds and flu, and all their attendant miseries were treated with the tea but it didn't end there. Poultices of the mixture were used for sprains, aches etc in the joints; also for boils, carbuncles and "gathered" fingers – whitlows and such. You could bathe your face in it to get rid of freckles, your eyes if they were sore or smarting. Sores on legs or arms were also bathed with the liquid.

Elderberries were very favoured too (perhaps it should be explained to the uninitiated that"ellum-blow" is the flower of the elder – is this a Forest dialect word?). The berries were boiled up with sugar, strained, and the resulting syrup was bottled and used in winter for coughs and colds. Strangely, the berries were always referred to as elderberries and only the flower was "ellum-blow". There is not a Forester alive over the age of 60 who does not know about ellum-blow tea. It seemed to be the universal panacea; thankfully the only use it didn't have was for constipation. Had it been so I can picture our childhood being one long-drawn-out consumption of EBT and we would undoubtedly have been less than grateful to the Lord who created this particular medicine "out of the earth".'

THE DOCTOR

'Before the NHS most families at Falfield belonged to a friendly or benefit society for a minimum monthly subscription to cover medical problems. The doctor from Thornbury occasionally called on horseback wearing hunting pink on his way to a meet.'

OPENING THE COTTAGE HOSPITAL

'I recall the opening of Winchcombe Cottage Hospital in 1928. The local people were asked to donate provisions to the hospital twice a year. The shopkeepers and traders would give, say, sacks of sugar and flour while the ordinary people would give jars of jam and preserves. Thousands of eggs were given and preserved in waterglass. Many of the local women walked to Corndean Hall (about two miles away) to work on the stitching and sewing of new curtains and furnishings for the hospital because their own homes were too small to accommodate the scale of the work! Everyone paid a "sub" to the Hospital Fund. It was collected by Mr Roberts of Rushley Lane, a local Sunday school teacher. You were always treated in an emergency at the hospital regardless of your payment record.'

The three ambulances that covered Cheltenham and the surrounding district in the 1930s, managed jointly by the St John Ambulance Brigade and the Red Cross.

SCARLET FEVER

'A sore throat, a temperature, and scarlet all over: time to call the doctor. Diagnosis – scarlet fever. In no time at all I was whisked off to the isolation hospital in the "fever" van. This was a horse-drawn vehicle similar to a Black Maria, totally enclosed except for a small skylight in the roof, through which I would occasionally catch a glimpse of grey sky or a waving branch as I lay wrapped up in a horrible hairy blanket, while the horse clip-clopped from the top of Chalford where we lived, down the steep Coppice Hill, and along the valley through Stroud to the hospital at Cashes Green, some four or five miles away.

As it was November, it was almost dark when I arrived and I was whisked into a bed and pushed into a little niche in the dimly lit boys' ward, the girls' ward being chock-a-block. They must have guessed I was a bit of a tomboy and preferred the boys to the girls! The whole of Chalford village seemed to be there, so there were many familiar faces in spite of being various shades of scarlet and I immediately borrowed a comic from the neighbouring bed, only to have it snatched out of my hand by an irate dragon of a sister – no reading for a week! No parents were allowed in the hospital; they could only peer at us through the windows, which made communication a little difficult, especially when you didn't know at which window the head would appear.

The usual length of stay was six weeks but owing to some dear little soul presenting me with ringworm I was there for four months including Christmas. Although only seven or eight, I was so enraged at seeing my friends going home after the allotted six weeks, I decided to lodge my own protest and I did it by wetting the bed. However, it did me no good as there were no clean sheets and no sympathy, and I was left to wallow in my misery.

Eventually I returned home, my adventures with scarlet fever etched on my memory for ever.'

Born At Home

'After the birth of my son in 1940, I was bound up like a trussed chicken and not allowed to even sit up for the next five hours. No hot drinks and nothing solid to eat. For the next three days I was only allowed to sit up to feed the baby, the rest of the time I had to lie flat on my back. After the first three days I could sit up but I was not allowed to get out of bed. Only my husband and my mother were allowed in the room as it was not considered right to have any visitors for the first week as this might upset me and I would not be able to breastfeed the baby. I had never been made such a fuss of before.

When the confinement was all over, I had to pay the nurse £1 10s, and my mother who looked after me £1. This was thought to be fair at that time.

Six weeks after the baby was born, you and the baby went to see the doctor and if all was well, you were told that things could now get back to normal.'

'In 1952 I came to Cinderford as a qualified midwife. We had a gypsy encampment nearby. They were a fine bunch of people – clean and tidy. One night I delivered a baby in a caravan. I wondered where the other children were. As soon as the baby cried, four little heads popped out from under the bed – that was

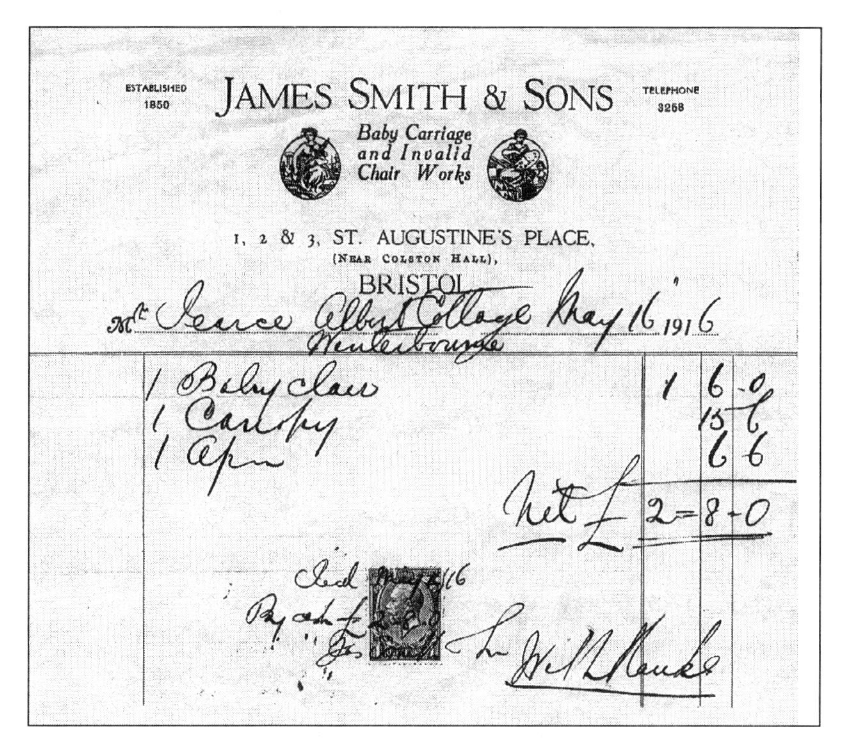

ESTABLISHED 1850

JAMES SMITH & SONS

TELEPHONE 3268

Baby Carriage and Invalid Chair Works

1, 2 & 3, ST. AUGUSTINE'S PLACE,
(NEAR COLSTON HALL),
BRISTOL

Mr Pearce Albert Cottage Winterbourne May 16 1916

	£	s.	d.
1 Baby chair	1	6	0
1 Canopy		15	6
1 Apron		6	6
Nett £	2	8	0

Preparing for the baby in 1916.

their sleeping quarters. After a quick peep at the baby, they went back again.'

'I was the district nurse at Churchdown in the 1940s, employed by the Gloucester County Nursing Association. During the war years a London family came to live at a house on the Green. One patient was expecting a baby after some years and was over 40 years old. I was with her during the night and it was bitterly cold. We decided to light a fire but the house was quite old and a deluge of soot came down the chimney. We stayed in the cold a few more hours, then we tried again. This time I had my share of soot, all over my gown, cap and mask. Later on a young doctor came and the patient had a forceps delivery. We were both very tired but pleased. I had a shock when I looked in a mirror though – my face was all black with soot.'

Name of Subscriber Mrs Gardner Resthaven the Pound

This Card must on no account be lost.

SUBSCRIPTIONS.

Minimum Family Subscription.—4/4 per annum or 1d. a week. This payment does not include wage earners over 16, or lodgers.

Subscribers of 10/- and upwards may avail themselves of the services of the Nurse, if required, in the same way as other subscribers.

Non-Subscribers.—2/- first visit, 1/- each subsequent visit. 10 consecutive visits will be regarded as a Subscriber for the remainder of that year.

Midwifery Fees.—

For Regular Subscribers	...	£1 5 0
For Non-Subscribers	...	£1 15 0

Maternity Fees.—

For Regular Subscribers	...	£1 0 0
For Non-Subscribers	...	£1 10 0

Miscarriages - Half-fees.

Unless Subscriptions are to-date, Non-Subscribers fees will be charged.

Date	Jan. 1939.	April 1939	July 1939	
Amount	1/1	1/1	1/1	
Collector	K. Hopkins	K Hopkins	K Hopkins	
Date	Oct –	Jan 1940	July 1940	
Amount	1/1	1/1	1/1	
Collector	K Hopkins.	K Hopkins	K Hopkins	
Date	Oct –	Jan 1941	April 1941	
Amount	1/1	1/1	1/1	
Collector	K Hopkins	K Hopkins	K Hopkins	
Date	July 1941	Oct 1941	Jan 1942.	April
Amount	1/1	1/1	1/1	1/1
Collector	K Hopkins	K Hopkins	K Hopkins	K Hopkins
Date	July 1942.	Oct. 1942.		
Amount	1/1	1/1		
Collector	K Hopkins	K Hopkins		

Many people paid regularly into a local Nursing Association before the NHS began in 1948.

'Babies were delivered at home at Leighterton either by the district nurse or a local woman. Several women recall that after having their babies in the 1940s and 1950s they could not go out of the house until they had been churched, a custom which now seems to have died out.'

THE LAST JOURNEY

'Long before the arrival of television, when wireless sets were in their infancy, village life would have been extremely dull had not everyone taken a great interest in events such as christenings, weddings and funerals.

Firstly, we knew something was afoot when the sexton, Oliver Smith, was seen approaching the church when everyone knew there was to be no service. We listened as he tolled the bell – a certain number (I believe it was 30 for a man – a lesser number for a woman), a short pause, and then the number denoting the deceased person's age. The muffled bell was eerie enough in the daytime but much worse on a dark winter's evening.

As we knew everyone in the village, it was easy to think of someone who'd been ill and say, "Poor old Tom (or Ellen) has gone at last", invariably adding for an old person, "it's a happy release". Hundreds of times I heard this remark.

Summer or winter, the bedroom window, where the deceased lay, was immediately opened wide to allow the spirit to escape. The district nurse *may* have been called on but only if the contribution (2d per fortnight taken to the village school) had been regularly paid to the "nurse's fund". However, in every village, there lived a handful of women whose spare time occupation was to sit with the dying (which they did most cheerfully) and then to lay them out so that relatives, friends and neighbours might view the corpse and say, "Didn't she look beautiful – just like a young girl", irrespective of her age!

The near relatives, however poor, felt compelled by convention to immediately go to town to buy funeral clothes – black dresses, coats and hats for the women; black ties for the men who usually found dark suits in their wardrobes, or a grey one with a black arm band. The women's black outfits were worn for six months or a year, followed by a period of half-mourning which was purple. My grandmother, after my grandfather's funeral, wore only black for the remainder of her life which was 18 years!

Edward Jenner of Berkeley
Pioneer in Vaccination
~Statue in Gloucester Cathedral~

On the funeral day all curtains were drawn, all blinds pulled down in every house on the route the cortege would take, as a mark of respect. Men, unwittingly caught in the street as the procession went by, doffed their hats and bowed their heads.

I well remember when the local undertaker acquired a wheeled bier. Until that time, the coffin had to be carried along a long path to the church door which provided such remarks as, "Poor old Harry was such a big man. He must have been heavy for the lads to carry." The men who attended the funeral dusted down their little-worn bowler hats which were compulsory funeral wear. The undertaker headed the procession in his top hat. After the service and the filing "two by two" to the graveside, when my grandmother always remarked "I shall be the next one" (we took no notice after she'd said it hundreds of times!), the mourners headed towards the deceased relatives' house for the funeral tea – the conventional home-boiled ham followed by home-made cakes and other delicacies which were enjoyed by all. Many remarked that Uncle Joe (or Aunt Mary) would not have wished them to be miserable and, after all, he/she had been always partial to a nice slice of ham when it was cooked at home.'

CHILDHOOD & SCHOOLDAYS

CHILDHOOD & SCHOOLDAYS

Carefree days are remembered from childhood, in times that were hard for many families but in which we enjoyed a freedom and simplicity of life and pleasures.

THE HEART OF OUR EXISTENCE

'When I was young in the early 1900s new babies came to our house with such regularity that it seemed I woke up every morning to the smell of carbolic and the nurse duly arriving complete with her little black bag. After a while she would let us see the new baby and although we were thrilled with the latest addition to our family, Mother was the more important person. After about three weeks we had the baby christened and Mother was churched also during the service, this being a thanksgiving for safe delivery. Gradually everything went back to normal – until the next time.

During my childhood we changed houses at least five times, each one a little bigger than the last. When the twins were born I shall never forget the first time I was allowed to take them out in the pram. I was sent into town to do some shopping and this particular shop had two entrances. Unfortunately I came out of the second door and, forgetting all about the twins, arrived home without them. It was only when Mother said, "Where are the twins?" that I realised they were still outside the shop. Stopping only long enough to gasp, "I knew I had something in my hands when I went out but couldn't think what it was," I ran back into town and retrieved them – fortunately they were still asleep.

We were always up to all sorts of tricks – climbing through the bedroom window into the garden to pick apples, when we were supposed to be in bed, or tying the sheets to the four corners of the brass bedstead and jumping off the top rail into the centre – poor Mother, I don't think she ever realised why the sheets had to be repaired so often. I can also remember dashing home from school one day and walking straight into the middle of a bread pudding that had been left to cool on the back doorstep.

Some time after the First World War we moved to Tuffley

Crescent and although the house was much bigger Mother could relax more as we were able to do so much more to help her. Dad was the provider, but Mother and the home were at the very heart of our existence; we each had our various tasks and conformed to a recognised pattern. The older ones cared for the younger ones, until such time as they could care for themselves. Such was the familiar pattern of our lives. On Sundays we attended church and no one was allowed to sew or do any unnecessary work during the day, it was a day of rest and quiet – if that was at all possible. We would often get fits of the giggles if someone said something funny, then Dad would have to threaten us with having no tea unless we stopped giggling.

What a lovely feeling Sunday always seemed to bring – everything clean and in our best dresses. I can still feel the thrill when I think of it.'

THE BLACKSMITH'S FAMILY

'I was born in 1914 in the little village of Maisemore and have lived there all my life, most of it at The Forge, as my father was the village blacksmith and also had a smallholding.

I was the eldest of four children and my memories of childhood are happy ones, although vastly different from today's children. We were expected to lend a hand with feeding animals, collecting eggs and blowing the bellows which kept the fire alight in the smithy. I was not tall enough to reach the handle and had to stand on the wooden box containing "The Mustard Nails" which were the ones used to nail the shoes to the horses' hooves. How my arms ached! I have memories of my father being wakened around 6 am on frosty mornings to put special nails in the shoes of the postman's horse to prevent it slipping. Blacksmith's Lane in front of the house was always full of farm implements waiting to be repaired. The busiest days were when new iron bands had to be fixed to the farm waggon wheels on the tyreing plate which was near our garden gate. We had few toys, but were the proud possessors of iron hoops made by my father and stamped with our initials. There was no electricity or running water. Aladdin lamps provided light and coal fire warmth.

The river Leadon (a tributary of the Severn) was quite near my home and was safe for bathing. It was there I learned to swim, as

Young Bill Cornock on his pony at Maisemore.

did many Maisemore children. Occasionally several families would get together for a picnic on High Redding Hill. At the summit was a wood and a spring – Scritch Scratch Well, all long since disappeared. My father had a fine bass voice and sang in the church choir for 50 years. Each Sunday he and his four offspring could be seen in the choir.

My twin brothers were famous for their escapades. As my mother often said, "What one does not think of the other does." Seldom a day passed without some mischievous act. My father made his own cider at his brother's cider mill. One day the twins found the key to one large cider cask, turned it on then threw the key away. We found them stark naked and bathing in a river of cider. Another occasion was when we found them in the fowls' house surrounded by "omelettes", having amused themselves by throwing eggs at one another. One Sunday morning, arrayed in their very best clothes, they seated themselves on my father's heap of slack coal which was used in the forge and threw it over one another until they were buried except for their heads.'

TWO UP, TWO DOWN

'Life began for me in cold December, two days after Christmas 1926. I shared two-up, two-down Haskins Cottage, Taynton, with my parents, one sister and three brothers, five fields from the road. Here I spent my first ten years. Growing up was a fun time for us, living where we did, so much to enjoy. We had four ferrets which we used to catch rabbits, the pigeons we trapped as they landed on the kale; we picked mushrooms and blackberries, and collected dry cow-pats for burning on the fire to help stretch the coal supply. Coal was never delivered to the cottage, we had to collect it from the roadside gate. In winter when the pond was frozen we placed lighted candles in jam jars on the ice so that we could see where to skate during the hours of darkness. "Mad Jack", that's what we called Mr Bradley the butcher, would throw pennies into the grass for us to find if we held the gate open for him to drive his horse and trap straight through to deliver at the Drews Farm.

When Mother went shopping we watched from a tree until the bus came then we ran down the fields to help carry the groceries. In summer she would hang the cheese, butter and meat in a bucket down the well to keep it cool. The well was several hundred yards away from the cottage so we had a long way to fetch water, especially if it was raining.

My father was gardener and my two sisters were in service for Mrs Bedford at Ryelands House, Taynton. Later he moved to Taynton House with the Misses Athertons and later still to Mr House at Hownhall Farm, when his Christmas box was a lovely fat goose.

School was at the now Parish Room at Taynton. It closed in 1934 and we then went to Tibberton and on to Newent. I often skipped school. Mother was most put out when the School Attendance Officer arrived to see where I was. Usually I was helping on the farm; I loved the horses.

All this ended in 1936, when we moved to 5 Wynford Villas, Taynton because the cottage was condemned for human habitation. It still stands but is used for storage. We could now play with more children in the road with whip and top, fish in the Wynford brook and play havoc in everyone's gardens. Then the war came, we all grew up and went our different ways.'

Days Out With My Grandfather

'Like so many other men in the early 1920s my grandfather was out of work and earned a little money by selling fish around the village and collecting rags from the larger houses and the "elite" of the neighbourhood, which, after being sorted to see if anything could be worn, were taken to the local flock mills to be washed and dried and, I imagine, made into flock for mattresses.

In 1924 he surprised everyone by moving to another village where he opened up a small drapery shop selling a variety of articles as well as drapery, which was in due time –

Quiet roads and the safety to roam – Swindon Lane, Southam in 1933.

unfortunately not in his lifetime – to grow into an emporium selling innumerable items which were apparently unobtainable elsewhere!

He owned a pony and cart, and in the early days would leave his wife in charge of the shop and set off to the outlying villages with suitcases full to overflowing with items of clothing and, in those days "unmentionable" but necessary articles for the country folk – mostly ladies who were unable to travel to the nearest town to shop except on rare occasions, perhaps at Christmas or in order to pay their Co-op bills.

In the early days of the shop I was about seven or eight and I used to spend quite a lot of my school holidays there.

When Grandfather went out on his rounds he would take me with him. How proud I was to be sitting with him, high up on the front of the cart, to see and be seen by everyone we happened to meet and to be introduced to all his customers as "my granddaughter". At most of the houses where we were invited in (a lot of the menfolk were disabled and housebound from the First World War and liked to have someone to talk to), I would be given a biscuit or a piece of cake and a drink of lemonade or dandelion pop.

Grandfather liked his beer and at lunchtime we would stop at one of the village pubs – and there were many of them – where he was always welcome, but in those days of course, children weren't allowed in, there being only a bar and no other rooms, so I was left outside with the pony and Grandfather would bring me an enormous cheese sandwich and a bottle of ginger beer, usually one with a marble in the top. There I would wait until he had drunk his fill and if it was winter, on emerging from the pub he would make me get down from the cart and swing my arms vigorously to get warm before starting for home. If he had imbibed a little too well we would amble gently home, the rhythmic clip-clop of the pony's hooves making us both a little sleepy and, apart from the occasional "Come on, boy" from Grandfather, the pony seemed to find its own way home.

Wonderful memories ... the mixed smell of ponies and leather and cheese sandwiches bring back vivid recollections of a dearly loved, military-looking grandfather with kiss-curls on his forehead which I loved to twirl – and he never said a word!'

A Child In The 1920s

'I was born in Tewkesbury in the 1920s and had four brothers. There wasn't much money as Dad didn't have a regular job but was a very keen fisherman. He made his own fishing nets, knitting them with string in the kitchen where we all lived because that was the only room with a fire, a black range which Mother had to black-lead and shine. Always a kettle boiling on the top, a stew simmering or boiled brisket. Herrings or bloaters were grilled on the front trivet and the large oven was never empty. Mother used to cook five individual milk puddings for us – rice, tapioca, sago, semolina or macaroni. Beautiful rabbit pies or stews, stuffed belly pork, eels or lamprey pie which of course Father caught.

The fire was kept going mostly with wood Father got from the river banks; he would collect it in his boat. Father used to sell fishing bait – maggots, worms and stale bread, which was bought cheap from the baker's and put in the bottom of the oven until it was brick hard and then broken down with a large hammer very fine. Father sold his eels for 9d a pound. He also used to send them in crates on the train to London market. When the baby eels (elvers) were in season I used to have to go round the houses asking people if they would like some, 6d a pint, take the basin and return with it. If I was lucky I would get a halfpenny and go to the old lady who sold home-made peppermint toffee sweets, they were lovely.

Toys were very few and Christmas meant one of Mother's stockings with an orange, apple, nuts, a few sweets and a silver 3d bit wrapped up in the toe. One year my mother made me a doll out of a black stocking and it had calico buttons for its eyes. She also dressed it. It must have been a great effort because she made all our clothes, all out of grown-up clothes, even the boys' trousers and she used to say, "I wish I could make shoes."

Mother tucked us all up in bed every night and in the winter we each had a brick (which had been in the range oven) wrapped in paper and then in a blanket to keep us warm. All was well until it fell out of bed in the middle of the night.

Indoor games were ludo, snakes and ladders, donkey or pen and paper but outdoor games seemed to come in seasons. It was safe to play on the streets, games like marbles, whip and top, hoops, rounders and skipping with an orange rope that reached from one side of the street to the other. We also went down on the Ham to play, and made lovely dens after haymaking. I'm sure the days were longer or it stayed lighter longer then.

CAREFREE DAYS

'The weather in the 1930s seemed to follow a pattern. At Eastertime it was perhaps rather cold with occasional frost but during summer months there seemed to be weeks of hot sunshine with the occasional thunderstorm which cleared the air. A storm used to last for all of three quarters of an hour with constant sheet-lightning and a real torrent of rain to accompany it. After an hour the sun would come out and it would be all fresh and green after the downpour. Then we had fine days to follow without any rain to speak of. August was the holiday month and I can remember weeks of hot sunshine when I and my school friend would go out all day in the woods and fields taking a picnic lunch.

Our parents never had to worry about us being harmed in those days – it was very carefree. A party of us used to go over to a farm in Cranham, a neighbouring village, where there was a lake for swimming. We would stay all day and if we had enough energy would walk up the steep hill to Miserden where Prothero's Bakery was. We would buy small crusty loaves and on the way home would pick at these to appease our hunger. I never had any left when I got home. We also used to have small tins of cocoa and sugar and would dip fingers in and suck them – mmm... quite refreshing. In season a stick of rhubarb was secreted in a picnic bag together with a jar or tin of sugar and we would dip the rhubarb in the sugar and eat it raw! We did not seem to come to any harm. We also tried to smoke dead sticks of honesty, which has many tubes in its formation, but the resultant smoke used to be so pungent that it made you cough and splutter.'

WAR BABY

'My birth should have coincided with D-day but, creating a precedent for life, I was late and didn't arrive until the 22nd June 1944. At that time, my father was serving in the Army in North Africa and Italy, seeing action at Cassino. I have no vivid recollection of his return but have been told that I would have nothing to do with this strange man. My parents had been married the previous year but Mum had continued to live at home with my grandparents who rented a house on the Cheltenham Road opposite the Double Gloucester public house.

My grandmother taught me how to make pastry with Trex – she always used a glass bottle filled with water as a rolling pin. She never hung out the washing, which had been boiled and blue-rinsed, unless she put on a hat – whatever the weather. When getting ready for bed, a brass bedstead with feather mattress, she would unpin the tight bun at the nape of her neck and brush her waist-length hair with an ivory-backed brush. She wore her pink, boned corset over the top of her vest and was always replacing the suspenders. She washed Grampy's shirts by hand but the collars were sent each week to the laundry to be starched. "One collar and two studs" stood me in good stead when spelling "necessary" in later years. Gran also taught me to knit and sew, and how to make wool balls using the carefully washed cardboard milk bottle tops from Sivells Dairy.

When Dad finally came back home, things did not work out too well with us all under the same roof. We were offered a room with Dad's cousin, his wife and daughter and it was from this address that I started school at Hatherley Infants. This didn't last long and we were allocated a Hawkesley bungalow, a pre-fab in Seventh Avenue, Tuffley. These were erected as a temporary measure for families like ours but some are still in use today. This was the height of luxury to us! I had my own bedroom and the kitchen contained a refrigerator and a stove which would burn anything and keep the kitchen warm.'

GAMES, TREATS AND CHORES

Games were played in their seasons, usually using the road as our playground and with the minimum of equipment. Spending our meagre pocket money at the sweet shop was a delight – but there were always chores to do at home.

When the street was the playground – Victoria Street, Cheltenham in 1930.

THE GAMES WE PLAYED

'Being a girl, street games in the 1930s at Tewkesbury were whip and top, yo-yos and hoops; the boys had marbles and cards to play pitch and toss, and small metal bombs which you opened up and put a cap inside and then when it was dropped it went off with a bang.'

'The local policeman at Charlton Kings in the 1920s knew and was known by everyone. He came around on foot to check on many things and would have a short conversation with the grown-ups. One day he told my father that there was a lot of bad coinage in circulation and asked to see the coins in Pa's pocket. He then picked out certain silver coins saying, "Thank you very much, these will do for the police charity." He told small boys off for playing games in the street. Our road was tree-lined so it was very convenient for using as a cricket pitch, with the stumps roughly chalked on the trees. This was frowned on by the policeman. The boys would keep an eye out for him while they were playing a "match". The cry would go up "RLCC" (Run Lads, Copper's Coming) as the policeman appeared and the small boys disappeared very quickly.

Other street games included hopscotch, hoops, top and whip and skipping which was seasonal. As if by magic one game,

On the banks of the river Leadon, with a bottle of pop.

having lasted a few weeks, was no longer played. The next fashion appeared and soon everyone would be equipped for it. Possibly because the village shop was selling the necessary items at the time, along with the aniseed balls, liquorice bootlaces and gobstoppers.

Another game was bug-in-the-hole, where you scooped out holes in the grass verge and bowled marbles or small pebbles into them. Each hole scored a pre-set number and each player had a fixed number of marbles. This was harder than it looked as the marbles bounced out again, it was quite a game of skill.

Most of the games were played by the boys, but sometimes I was allowed to join in, possibly when my mother had some chocolate biscuits to spare.

The boys made a dug-out in the garden next to ours. It had a fireplace where they attempted some primitive and inedible cooking. It had a tarpaulin roof – borrowed no doubt – and boxes to sit on. The boys "smoked" clay pipes with tobacco made from dried bean leaves. Girls were most privileged to be allowed to climb down into this male territory.'

'As a child in the late 1930s my home was in Church Street, Tewkesbury, near the Abbey. There was a long narrow yard at the back of the house with just enough space for skipping and ball games and for Dad to fit a swing in the doorway of the washhouse. When Ella and her family moved to a house opposite we soon chummed up as we attended the same school. Although there was little playing space around the houses we were fortunate that it was safe for us to play together in the neighbourhood.

Our special places were the Victoria Pleasure Gardens and on the Ham. The Pleasure Gardens was an area of lawn, paths and small bushes and had once also contained a Crimean War cannon and a bandstand (removed for scrap as part of the war effort!). A flight of steps led down to the river. This part of the river was quite shallow and there were some small islands covered in scrub and willow trees, a fantastic place for hide and seek and the building of dens in the summer months. And of course we paddled in the river and explored the islands. The Ham is the large meadow between the rivers Avon and Severn. It is crossed by a network of paths and was a great place for walks, wild flowers such as lady's smock and buttercups and listening to the skylarks and corncrakes. When the grass had been cut for hay the Ham became our playground, a site for games of rounders and cricket and the place where Mum taught me to ride a bike.

In early autumn our interest turned to roller skating – usually along the pavement between the Abbey gates and Abbey Terrace – there was a wall on one side to hold on to. But the best fun was to be had playing Fox and Hounds (a superior variety of hide and seek played in teams). The local alleys and small lanes were an ideal setting with gas lamps leaving areas of shadow where a cunning "fox" could hide while the "hounds" ran past.'

'The highlight of the year for the children of Southfield was the cutting of the grass in the recreation ground. We built houses and picnicked for days till the grass became hay and was collected.'

'Baler twine figured largely in my childhood in the 1950s. Then it was made of natural fibre (jute, probably) not the harsh synthetic twine of today. We plaited baler twine to make thicker rope, just right for climbing, making swings and lassoos. It was useful as the string for a bow. We would cut nut or willow (or was it ash?) sticks, shave the twigs off, notch each end and then bend and string the bow. Smaller nut sticks were used for arrows, pointed at one end and notched at the other. Pull it back and twang; watch the arrow fly. Occasionally we attempted to slot feathers in the end, but it was better to have 20 plain arrows to fire off than one painstakingly flighted arrow.

Baler twine was used to lash the wood together for our rafts. These were wood and oil drum constructions that we floated on the pond in the fields. The fun was in the building of them, rather than the paddling; we would spend days at a time building and improving a raft.

Then, as now, our play was influenced by television – mostly by cowboys and Indians like *The Lone Ranger* and *Bronco*. I developed a good lassoo technique from watching *The Lone Ranger*, and could lassoo a post from several yards. Once, I remember, the vivid images of lassooed steers proved too much to resist, and I lassooed one of the young cattle in the covered yard. It dashed off, I dared not let go, and it dragged me all round the yard through the straw bedding. After that, I always considered the consequences before letting fly with the lassoo!'

'Out of school at Stroud in 1930 we played in the fields, running up and down the banks, and picked flowers in the woods. We would tie a rope to the railings and skip, or play hide and seek. The boys used to make trolleys on old pram wheels and handwarmers out of cocoa tins with holes pierced in the sides and string as a handle over the top – there was a piece of rag inside which they lit and which usually smelled horrible! The boys also played conkers – "obbley, obbley, conkers".

Sweets and Treats

'Rosie Anna's was a favourite shop to call in on the way to school at Stow on the Wold in the 1930s. They sold all kinds of small sweets in three-cornered bags for a halfpenny – raspberry and lemon drops, sherbert dabs with liquorice sticking out, love hearts with messages on, edible eggs with small gifts inside, and huge gobstoppers which changed colour as they were sucked and examined quite often with grubby fingers. Marbles of all sizes could be found in wonderful colours.'

Playing in the river Severn at Framilode in 1943.

'My most treasured memory of Brimscombe as a child in the late 1920s and early 1930s was of our local village shopkeeper. Oh, what patience he had with us.

When we were given our penny pocket money, we had to put a halfpenny in a money box to save and the other halfpenny we clutched in our hot little hands and raced off with it to the tiny shop which sold everything from bacon to paraffin.

"Ha'penny out the box, please, Mr Beard", we'd say politely.

From under the counter he would bring a shallow box, roughly two feet square, divided into sections and covered with a white piece of paper pinned along the top edge.

With great ceremony he would lift the white paper, and what a feast met our wide eyes. Now, should we choose a liquorice bootlace or pipe, or some gobstoppers, coconut tobacco, candy cigarettes or should we blow the whole halfpenny on a lucky dip packet or a sherbet fountain?

After much thought we decided. How we savoured those delicacies and tried to make them last as long as possible. It would be a whole week before we got any more.'

'When I was a young girl I used to walk to Willersley school past the little general shop with its pretty bow window, its iron railings and gate, and a fuchsia in the garden.

The shop was kept by one Nanny Franklin, an old spinster lady with a sharp tongue and soft heart. I remember all those long years ago passing the shop on my first day at school. I was just five years old and of course the shop was a great attraction for my brother and me.

Nanny sold all sorts of things, especially sweets, and you could buy a bar of chocolate for a ha'penny. Most of the sweets were twopence a quarter.

Nanny Franklin could be a bit frightening when she was cross. You could see past the counter into the living quarters, and as soon as you set foot in the shop she would totter out with a sharp, "Now then, what do you want? And keep your grubby hands off my clean counter." And clean it was, squeaky clean, with gleaming bottles of sweets and highly polished brass scales and weights, shining as brightly as her bright blue eyes.

My brother and I, partners in crime and always up to mischief, decided to test Nanny's patience – always a risky thing to do. I, muggins, was to go into the shop on our way home from school and ask for an ounce of humbuggers, a naughty word to use in those days. My goodness me! Wasn't she cross, and didn't she shout at me. "Be off with you, and wash your mouth out with carbolic soap." I was so scared I beat a hasty retreat, my brother as usual being nowhere to be seen. When I got home I had to change my bloomers.

We used to gather cowslips and dandelions for Nanny to make into wine, and she would always give us a sweet each out of one of the big glass jars. Unfortunately after she died it was never the same again. Her brother, who inherited the shop, was not quite so hygienically minded as his sister, and it soon deteriorated and closed down.

But the shop is still there with its pretty bow window, the fuchsia and the iron railings. The railings and gate must have been overlooked when ironwork was collected during the war and melted down to make munitions. I don't think my little granddaughter would get many humbuggers for a ha'penny these days. And she probably wouldn't get shouted at either!'

'Mrs Stephens kept the sweet shop at Lechlade. She used to put all the broken bits together and sell a bag full for a halfpenny. The children loved them!'

Nutting

'Early in October in the 1900s, we were given two days' holiday from Sapperton school to gather hazel nuts. Mothers would prepare a meal for us to take – cake, sandwiches, cold tea and lemonade – and aunts and cousins accompanied us. We carried crooks made of bent sticks to reach the tallest branches. The keepers and woodmen told us where the best nuts could be found.'

Chores To Be Done

'I was one of nine children and we lived in the small village of Cliffords Mesne. When the children of our family came home from school, the hay for the horses had to be cut (my father was a horse dealer). This had to be done every night, as my father went away during the week in an old caravan, supplying hay for horses. We also had to wash our own socks and stockings and we all had other jobs to do. There wasn't time to get bored.'

'My mother vividly recalls that when she was a young girl she had a paper round – with a difference. She had to walk to Longhope station to collect the *Gloucester Journal* and then walk back to May Hill. This was just the start. When she arrived back on the hill, her job of delivering commenced and all for the love of it, no pay whatsoever!'

SCHOOLDAYS – THE BEST YEARS OF OUR LIVES?

Long walks to school, wet clothes drying by the stove or open fire, large classes of all ages, strict discipline both in and out of school – memories of village schools through half a century.

A VICTORIAN HEADMASTER

'My grandfather John Blowen was a Victorian headmaster. On Sundays the Blowen children were sent out to deliver dinners to poor widows, this before they could have their own meal. He was sorry for children who had to leave school at an early age to work on the farms and in the large houses as servants. Two evenings a week after school and when these boys came home from work, he walked to Frampton Mansell to continue with their lessons. These lessons were held in a shed lent by a farmer, the boys paying one penny each for candles to light the room.'

A LONG TREK HOME

'We lived on the edge of Tibberton in the early 1900s and my sister Rose and I walked to school each day – some four miles over the fields and past the mill if dry. As lessons did not end until four o'clock it was a long trek home in the dark during the winter months.'

Children at Ebley school in 1918, gardening during lesson time.

VERY STRICT

'Mr Garner was a very good teacher, but strict. He would set us to work and then walk outside and watch through the windows to see if we were misbehaving – and woe betide anyone who did! However, I only remember one boy being caned in front of the school and he had played truant for three days (unheard of then). His father had followed him into school to give permission for him to be caned. Billy was a devil-may-care, *Just William* type of boy, but that punishment calmed him down. Other pupils who misbehaved were taken out of the classroom to be caned or sent to stand in the corner.

I remember the rhyme we sang when skipping:

Mr Garner is a very nice man
Tries to teach us all he can.
Reading, writing and arithmetic,
But doesn't forget to use the stick.
But disobey, disobey. Naughty girl to disobey.'

SAPPERTON SCHOOL

'I was a little girl at Sapperton Church of England school (which was built by Earl Bathurst) and this is how I remember our day was spent. The bell was rung at 8.50 am and if fine we stood in

Blaisdon schoolchildren in the 1920s.

lines to march into school; if wet we hung our cloaks and went into class. Girls and infants hung cloaks in one porch, boys in the other. Prayers and a hymn were sung, then the sliding doors closed for the infants' separate lessons. Until 9.45 am it was Scripture, reading from the bible, learning new hymns and the catechism, then the register was called. Arithmetic was always the first lesson of the day, followed by English, History, Geography, reading until twelve o'clock with a break for playtime at 10.45 am. Grace was sung at noon after the Reverend Cropper came in, then we had to curtsey, saying each time, "Good morning Sir, Good morning Miss, Good morning Teacher."

At 1.20 pm we returned for afternoon lessons. Grace was sung and every day tables chanted in a sing-song way and then tables of measurement, liquids etc. These were usually found printed on the backs of exercise books. The remainder of the afternoon was spent learning poetry, or painting and drawing for the boys, the girls sewing pinafores, knitting socks, making samplers in cross stitch etc. with a break at 2.45 pm for afternoon playtime. A small cupboard on the wall contained reading books which were allowed on Friday afternoons for those who had done good work during the week. A large map of the world hung on the classroom wall and it showed the British Empire. A wall chart told us the story of the Gloucestershire Regiment, its battles and its honours.

The school was heated by pipes around the walls, in winter the mornings were cold and by afternoon too hot. We sat in desks for four children. The infants consisted of Baby Class, Second Class Infants and Standard I, with Standards II to V in the "big" room. The girls went to school in red cloaks provided by Countess Bathurst. She also gave the boys navy blue jerseys.

Because Mr Midwinter's cottage had very little garden, his wife was allowed to hang her washing on the village green. As the school playground was small and our grassy banks at the back were the gardens, the older children were allowed on the green to play cricket. When the wind was blowing the washing well it was considered to be an even greater sport to try to throw the cricket ball into the billowing legs of Mrs Midwinter's knickers!'

Without Shoes

'Some children in Miserden came to school without shoes. All the children enjoyed the severe winters when ponds and rivers froze, but they suffered greatly with chafed legs.'

Keeping Dry

'Many children at Stow on the Wold infants' school in the 1930s did not own wellingtons, and often only wore gym shoes or daps all the year. Sometimes socks would be hung on the radiators, so the children could put them on dry to go home in. An elderly lady would regularly arrive at school when it rained, with a clothes basket full of coats which she lent to children who did not have one. These were returned the following day. Some boys had overcoats made from their fathers' short coats. Long trousers were not worn until a boy was a teenager.'

A Miner's Child

'My first memories of village life in St Briavels go back at least 63

Pupils at Stone school in about 1922.

years. I was then about two years old. My father was a coal miner in South Wales. From what my mother told me conditions in the mines then were very bad and many miners came up from Wales seeking work in the Forest of Dean mines. We moved into a small cottage up Front Street as it was then called. Opposite us was the village police station. The cellar there was occasionally used to sober up any drunks who had strayed in from neighbouring villages. The village school was, and still is, at the top end of the village. In winter it was always very cold in the playground. Any heating inside the school was from closed-in coal burning stoves. Very temperamental things. If the school caretaker had not got them going before classes started, that would be it. We had to put up with being cold.

The headmaster and his wife lived in the school house which was attached to the school. On Monday mornings the headmaster was usually in a bad mood. I found out in later years that he always had to light the fire underneath the copper boiler and fill it with water ready for the weekly wash.

There were no school dinners! Children who lived near went home for lunch from twelve until 1 pm. Children from the Common either brought sandwiches or went to the village bakery opposite the school. They were able to buy a freshly baked bap, a nub of butter, and a chunk of cheese. We all had a small bottle of milk during our first play time break. Many of the children who lived outside the village had several miles to walk to school each day.'

SCHOOL AT RODMARTON

'I started at Rodmarton village school in 1935, at the age of four and a half, and my most abiding memory of the infants department is having a sleep at lunchtime on a folding canvas bed! The headmaster was a Mr Webb and once we moved to the juniors he caned us for all sorts of trivial reasons such as talking, getting a sum wrong and so on. We had a walk of a mile and a half each way to school and when school meals started we had them in the village hall at a cost of 1s 8d a week.'

THROUGH THE STANDARDS

'I was nearly six years old in 1927 when I started school at Westbury on Severn. We had to walk from "The Heald" in the Rodley Road. I remember being late on a very cold frosty morning, and being sent to sit at the back of the class by Miss West, the strict but very efficient infants teacher. She eventually took pity on my tears and let me warm my hands by the open fire which was the only form of heating.

By the time I proceeded to Standard I, I could read well and do simple arithmetic, which was always my favourite subject. We were then taught by Miss Hart and Miss Watkins, and I realise now just how well they taught us, and what a vast number of subjects they had to cover. Being left handed I was often made to sit on my own and write with my right hand, which I found almost impossible. Needless to say, I quickly changed to my left hand as soon as the teacher turned back to the rest of the class. Every morning we were taken out to do physical exercise which was known as "drill", and which most of us enjoyed. At winter playtimes the teachers made cups of cocoa which we could buy for ha'penny for our mid morning break. Two of us were then allocated to wash the cups in the small sink in the cloakroom, where everyone washed their hands!

By the time I reached Standard III Miss Greening was our

teacher; and what a good foundation she laid for our future lives. We read many of Shakespeare's works and acted out quite a few of them. We also studied poetry by many of the famous poets; ancient history about all the Greek heroes; and one of my favourites: "Picture Study", where we passed around pictures of great paintings (which were all in sepia, not colour) and then wrote about them. We were also taught to knit, sew well, and to use a sewing machine. We were shown too how to draw and paint; and to crown all, this *one* teacher (who was not at all an athletic type) had to take us out and teach us to play netball and rounders. We also did country dancing. Looking back I just cannot imagine how she coped with it all, while still keeping our respect and interest.

The highlight of our year was when Mr Kelly, the good and kindly vicar of the time, took all of the children, with the help of our teachers, to the top of Popes Hill on Ascension Day. We had a marvellous time – taking a picnic meal and happily picking foxgloves with no idea that they were very poisonous.

By the time I got into the "top class", Mr Eaton had come as headmaster. He was a very impatient man who wielded the cane for the slightest reason. I remember how hard he was on a girl who was deaf. I was supposed to be his pet, yet I had the cane on my hands three times for talking in class. One good thing that he did do was to teach as many of us as he could to swim. The brook at Westbury (opposite Westbury Court) had just been cleared out and a concrete base laid below the waterfall. We changed in a cow shed and then plunged into the very icy water.

We also learnt cookery in a caravan in the school grounds. I used to cook a lunch which my sister shared. We were even shown how to wash clothes properly and how to keep a kitchen clean.'

'When I was at school one or two of the village schools were beginning to close. I remember children coming from Redmarley, Lowbands and also from Cliffords Mesne. Boys came from May Hill – they were very rustic compared with the Newent people and they wore big heavy boots. I remember one teacher saying that their boots were a pound of leather with six pounds of nails on the bottom.

We played out in a hard stone yard. The boys were very cruel. The big ones used to get hold of the little boys and make them do things. I can remember there were tortures and all sorts of things. There was a Chinese burn – screwing the wrists round with two hands, one going one way and one the other, which made the skin burn and was very painful. There was another one which was probably a more modern type of thing where they got a large magnifying glass from an old-fashioned flashlight and when it was a hot sunny day, they would get hold of one of the boys, hold his arms and let the sun concentrate through the magnifying glass and burn the hand and made the boy scream. Later in the school, they took a piece of coke from the coke shed and rubbed it up the back of the neck and of course it used to catch the hairs. In the summer they would hold a boy's arms down and spread dried lawn cuttings over his face. It was impossible to put one's hands up to the face and this was another little hardship we endured.

We used to get together naturally in small groups and sang rhymes such as "The Big Ship Sails on the Ally Ally Oh"; "Oranges and Lemons" was another one where two people held their arms up and linked hands and everyone passed underneath the arch. At the end, the unlucky ones had their heads "chopped off" to "here comes a chopper to chop off your head." "Ring a Ring a Roses" was another favourite, the origins of which probably go back to the days of the Plague.

There were some big gardens at Picklenash School at that time and the older boys were allowed to have plots of their own and learned to plant seeds and grow vegetables. Competitions were organised and the gardens were beautifully kept too. That was a rather nice feature of the school but, of course, when the school needed more space in later years, all this came to an end. That training gave the boys an opportunity to know the soil as many would have gone straight on to farms. The playgrounds were quite big but none of them had a sealed covering; they were all just the bare sand that had always been there. When the wind blew we used to get terrific sandstorms. The sand used to get into the school as well – it blew through the doors. There were extra internal doors to make the school warmer which stopped some of the sand, but it used to get into our shoes and clothes and when we were fighting or playing we rolled about in it. Most children caught impetigo soon after they started school, which was caused by a soil-borne organism, and had to have time off school but subsequently became immune and didn't get it again. The impetigo was painted with a sort of purple dye. When I was small most children were vaccinated against smallpox, the needles leaving a mark where they went into the skin.

The headmaster's name was Mr Hudson, who lived to be a great age. He was a strict disciplinarian who lined boys up in front of the school and caned them. The cane was used very often. Boys who scrumped apples from a garden nearby and misbehaved outside school hours ensured Mr Hudson would get himself worked up prior to carrying out a caning.'

Strict Rules

'The winters were much colder! I remember at my first school the milk was put on the range to thaw out before we could drink it. The bottles had cardboard tops and were collectors' items as many different ones were produced during the year. The milk expanded when frozen and I have a mental picture of the cardboard top resting an inch above the neck of the bottle.

The classroom was run under strict rules and I remember having to practise writing and if I didn't keep my first finger straight down the pen, the finger was whacked with a ruler! I would have been nine at the time.

The toilets were certainly not up to today's standard – and that's an understatement. They were always "across the playground", always cold and always seemed to be protected from prying eyes by a partition of corrugated iron.

PT was compulsory and I remember coconut matting – that always rubbed the skin – and dare I say it, navy blue knickers with a pocket!'

At Grammar School

'I attended Tetbury grammar school during the war, from 1943 to 1947. The school consisted of two large houses fronting onto Long Street and backing onto The Chipping. There were 134 pupils, boys and girls.

The teachers were either very young or too old for active service, though after the war we had ex-servicemen and women join the staff after a government training scheme. The heating in the classrooms was by anthracite stoves, so you froze at the back and overheated at the front. We stayed in the classrooms for lessons and the teachers came to us, so when one didn't appear we had a good time. We also played the usual pranks such as lodging something on the top of the door to fall on the next poor soul who entered. School dinners were awful except on Fridays, when we had a choice.'

School Dinners

'School dinners were delivered ready cooked to Maisemore school in the 1950s. We had a dinner lady to serve them up and wash up afterwards. We queued to be served the main course and took it in turns to be dinner monitor and sit at the end of the long trestle table to serve the pudding and stack up the dirty plates and dishes. Dinners in those days cost five shillings a week and milk was free. The milk was kept in a crate outside the back door and froze solid in the winter.

Our head teacher was Miss Price. She used to suck Fox's Glacier Mints all day long which seemed most unfair to me

At Upton St Leonards in 1954.

because we were not allowed to eat sweets in class. But if Miss Price was pleased with you, she gave you a mint. I remember the heating stove in school – it used to glow bright red and the coal shed was next to the outside toilets.'

School in the 1950s

'When I started school at Lechlade in 1954 there were three classes with each pupil spending two years in each class. The youngest ones started their day with a prayer and a bible reading in their own classroom, while the other two classes had assembly together. The music for the hymns was provided by Mrs Tanner playing the piano with a group of children playing recorders.

The little ones then began their lessons with reciting the alphabet, learning letters and numbers and saying tables parrot fashion with the aid of an abacus. The older ones were doing sums as well, adding, taking away, times and long division, along with fractions, angles and pounds, shillings and pence.

Once a week the vicar came in and took scripture, when we learnt the catechism, bible stories and about church festivals. We walked down to the church several times a year for special services. All this took us up to playtime at mid-morning when everyone had their third of a pint of milk. After break we might have listened to a nature programme or *Singing Together* on the wireless or gone back to the playground for PT (physical training). For this we changed into black daps but kept our ordinary clothes on and we were each given a small rush mat to do our exercises on. At midday we had our dinner, which was brought from Cirencester in vacuum containers. A few children went home for dinner but none brought sandwiches. After this we had more playtime.

We started the afternoon with reading and writing or perhaps spelling. During the summer months we did country dancing or played stool ball or rounders. I remember once going to Cirencester to a dance festival with groups from other schools in the country. The girls in our group had made their gingham skirts at school and wore white blouses, the boys wore khaki shorts and white shirts with a wide maroon sash round their waists. Afternoons also included sewing for the girls and gardening for the boys. Other times we did painting,

College Court, Gloucester – home to the tiny house chosen by Beatrix Potter for her Tailor of Gloucester.

made models with paper, cardboard and plasticine. Once we did some very basic woodwork and made picture frames to take home.

We had yet another mid-afternoon playtime and then a short lesson and a prayer to end our day at school.'

A Special Smell

'School had a special smell, or at least a pot pourri of smells, and the older the school the more impregnated with them it is. Farmor's school had absorbed over two centuries of smells within its stout Cotswold stone walls before I joined the body of pupils who would, in turn, leave their own post-war whiffs among those of its Georgians and Victorians. To appreciate a smell one has to experience it – certainly there was nothing in the collection that could warrant the words "scent" or "fragrance" – except the momentary drifts of newly-mown grass from the adjacent churchyard in summer and the warm yeasty wafts of bread and lardy cakes cooking in Bill Radway's bakehouse borne on a sharp easterly air in winter.

Different areas of the school closeted their own special smells; once the big school door was opened it led us into a dark passageway which held the aura of dripping coats drying against dulled, painted stone walls; to the left was the woodwork room sharply spiced with freshly planed shavings, curled and wafer thin on the thickly planked floor; to the right was the Geography room which contained more of an atmosphere than smell in its rolls of canvas-backed maps, glazed globe and curly-edged charts of population distribution and rainfall. The old abacus, the dog-eared, grey-covered arithmetic books and yardstick (which also doubled as a pointer or ruler for the blackboard which had turned grey many years ago, and as a jammer open of hingeless windows) signalled its use as the Maths room, and the room also acquired a depth of odour from the single Bunsen burner and the limited range of chemicals kept on the widest topped cupboard which made it the Science room on Friday afternoons.

A flight of stone stairs led to the Cookery room – a haven of hot treacle and baked onions, leavened with the distinctive aroma of Brasso and vinegar on Tuesdays, when the "country girls" were brought in from neighbouring village all-age schools for Housecraft. The top classrooms were "all subject" so varied from the crisp freshness of checked gingham for school dresses during sewing lessons, to the dried up dampness of old books of parsing and punctuation and chronicles of the reigns of all the monarchs – their contents as dry as the dust in the tall cupboards in which they were stored in graduated rows according to size and shape rather than subject matter.

Over-riding all were the soporific scents of cough drops and eucalyptus-soaked hankies, vapour rub and chilblain salves, camomile lotion and the sickly smell of "Quassia chips" on heads declared "not clean" by the probing fingered School Nurse, and the cloying taste-smell of school milk warming in its third-of-a-pint bottles on top of the coke-fired pot-bellied stove as wet knitted gloves started to steam on the high iron fireguards.

All came together each morning when the school assembled to stand shoulder to shoulder, to hear the notices for the day and give praise in our thin high-pitched voices for its dawning and faith in what was to follow.'

The World of Work

The World of Work

Farming has changed so much over the past 50 years, since horses provided the power on the land and harvest and haymaking were a part of the lives of everyone who lived in the country.

Our Farm at Chipping Camden

'My parents' farm at Chipping Camden was mixed, having cows, sheep, pigs, cart horses, hens, ducks, and geese; the crops were wheat, oats, barley, hay, peas, sprouts, mangolds, apples, plums and cherries. The land was worked mainly with horses for ploughing and cultivation. My father bred cart horses and used to supply Fardons Vinegar Company in Birmingham with horses to pull the drays. They had names like Prince, Boxer, Duke, Nobby, Kit and Whitefoot. The pony that pulled the milk float was Dolly Grey.

Bonnie the cart horse taking out hay on a snowy morning near Blaisdon.

As children we went charlock pulling in the corn crops. Charlock has a yellow flower (rather like rape) and a hairy stem which could cause irritation. We also went stone picking on arable fields. We collected stones into heaps which were collected by horse and cart and used to mend potholes in the farm tracks. Any money we had, we had to earn.

We rode in the waggons at harvest to take tea to our father and also took our own tea to eat in the field. I remember the small bodied, long legged spiders, called harvestmen which ran about the bed of the waggons after unloading, also the black beetles called, I think, Devil's coachmen. When the cornfields were cleared it was the usual practice to take the poultry pens to the fields so that the hens could feed on the grain that had fallen on the ground. Farms usually had a certain amount of grassland near the village where the milkers were kept and some land on the hills for corn and other crops. When the hens were taken to clear up the corn there was always the job of walking about two miles to shut up the pens just before dark, because if the hens were not shut in, the fox would be sure to be round in the night.

Hay was cut and made, being turned a few times to dry it with horse-drawn tedder, raked into rows with a horserake and picked up loose to be stacked in ricks and thatched. In winter the rick was cut with a hay knife into kerves, (a kerf was about a three foot cube). The pitchfork was stuck firmly into the middle of the kerf and heaved over onto the head and shoulders. I remember seeing the cowman walking to the cow yard with a kerf of hay and all that could be seen below it were two legs and the handle of the fork.

The cows were shorthorn breed, and produced the milk for the milk round which delivered twice a day. The milk was in churns and drawn off into an oval two-gallon bucket with lid, which had a brass rail inside on which hung the measures, one pint and half pint. Milk was 3d a pint and cream was 6d a quarter pint. We had a hand-turned separator and the skim milk was fed to pigs along with home-ground barley meal. Surplus cream was made into butter. Churning was always done on Tuesdays, and the cream was kept in the cellar in large brown two-gallon earthenware jars to which was added salt. The salt came in large bars about two feet long and weighing several pounds, and was sawn up into pieces about the size of a large egg. The jars had to be stirred every day. When brining the butter the test for strength of the brine was to see if it would float an egg.

When peas were ready for picking local women came as well as itinerant families who lived rough in barns or even under hedges. They were called diddicoys. Peas went to market in unbleached cotton bags holding 20lbs of peas. These bags were often stolen by the itinerants if the weigher-up did not keep a check on how many had been issued. They cut a hole for the head and two armholes and thus had a vest. They were usually flea ridden and these would transfer to my father who was weighing up and they came home with him and then got on to us children. Beds were left covered to keep warm when we got up, and my mother would search them, carefully turning back the covers, armed with a moistened cake of soap to dab smartly when a flea was spotted, before it had time to jump. It was embedded in the soap and killed by crushing between two thumb nails.

In the autumn there was the annual lamb tailing done with a hot iron on a block of wood. The tails were brought to the house warm where my mother had boiling water ready; the tails were scalded one at a time and the wool plucked off. They were then made into lamb tail pie, a great favourite of my father though I don't recollect liking it much. Also we had a pig or two killed and there was a lot of work making lard (we liked the scratchings, the crispy bits after the leaf was rendered), backbone pie, brawn from the head, salting the sides and hams. Some fresh joints and liver were exchanged with neighbours and we had return joints when they killed their pig. I hated liver, still do, but we always had to eat everything and leave a clean plate, otherwise it was brought out at the next meal.'

HARD WORK

'In the late 1920s my father worked on the farm at Southam, while my mother did casual work. Until the Second World War, all the work was done with horses, then came the first tractor. All the milking was done by hand. In the summer the men were working till ten o'clock at night haymaking. For all this work they received £2 10s, which they got at Christmas.'

'In the 1940s farm work was physically hard. Horses were still in use although tractors were becoming more numerous. Corn was

Haymaking at Manor Farm, Southam in 1933, with Cleeve Hill in the background.

cut with a binder and the sheaves had to be stooked and left to dry. As the area of standing corn became smaller and smaller, the chance of rabbits darting out became greater. A rabbit made a great addition to meals in this time of rationing so not many managed to escape. Oats had to stand in stooks for three Sundays before being put into ricks.

When ready the sheaves were pitched up on to a waggon, taken to the rickyard and built into a rick – a skilled job. A badly made rick would collapse. Rain could not penetrate the walls of a rick and the top was waterproofed by thatching. When the farmer was ready to sell the corn, another hard and dirty job had to be done – threshing. The sheaves were fed into the top of the thresher and out from different openings came the corn, the straw and the chaff. As the rick neared its end, rats and mice might dart out, to be chased by waiting boys and dogs.

Each October we had a potato picking holiday from school. It was hard work but we children could earn ourselves some money.'

'I was one of a big family and left school at 13 to work for a farmer-butcher nicknamed "Bumper". His wage was 3s 6d per day and sometimes hours stretched to 10 pm.

I soon tired of Bumper and "bettered myself", as we used to say, by taking a job at Winchcombe Taryard. Working hours were six to six but I did have 5s per day and Saturday afternoons off. I used the half day to haul a handcart loaded with crates of bottled beer and stout from an off-licence store to householders all round the town.

Later on, when unemployed, the benefit was 3s 6d per day. So when we (my brother and I) were offered muck-spreading on Roel Farm, four miles away, we soon legged it up Sudeley Hill, taking our bottles of cold tea and bread and home-cured lard sandwiches with us. It was piece-work at halfpenny a heap and a cart-load made three heaps! By working like stink, we earned 4s 6d a day – a shilling more than the "dole". Men hated being unemployed and they would take any work offered, even if it was some miles away.

We used to leave home at 6 am to cycle to Dumbleton for a seven o'clock start on threshing work – it was still too dark for the farmer to see how many of us arrived! Later I spent some years on the Sudeley Estate, on Farmcote Wood Farm and Towl

Cleaning up the threshing machine in the 1920s at Packhurst Farm, Edge.

Farm and the wage was £2 with Saturday afternoon off.

Sometimes there was the chance of a day's beating and the lucky ones got to carry a cartridge bag for one of the shooting party. This usually meant a tip of 2s 6d to add to the day's pay of six to nine shillings, and a rabbit.

I also worked at Toddington Orchard Co and at the Hailes' Fruit Farm. The wage was 30s minus 9d insurance, so I moved on to a quarry, loosening stone with crowbars for £2 a week. Being "in the money" I popped the question and got married in 1936.'

NEW MOWN HAY

'The smell of new mown hay reminds me of the pre-war days of haymaking in the Forest, the beautiful Royal Forest of Dean. The day would start at around 6 am with a ride on a horse-drawn waggon through Baker's Piece, a winding lane with blackberry bushes on either side, and because we were travelling so slowly we could pick the blackberries as we swayed to and fro.

Very often we would see field mice hopping and scurrying in and out of the grass at the side of the road, and even rabbits running to get to the safety of their homes. All very exciting. Our lunch would consist of newly baked bread and cheese, and home-cooked bacon washed down with cider.

I don't think we were much help, all we seemed to do was fall about and hide in the hay and get very tired. But the smell of new-mown hay reminds me of long ago summers when each day had a clear blue sky and peace prevailed.'

MAKING BUTTER AND CHEESE

'Butter making in Gloucestershire has for many years been the product of farmhouses, where many different types of churns were used. My brother-in-law, Alvan Blanch, invented the Blow Churn, which blew air into the cream by electricity. There were

Early cars had a variety of uses – including getting in the hay!

glass churns, with beaters, and wooden churns. My mother used one of the latter.

The cream used for butter making was skimmed from the milk, set up in wide shallow pans when the milk was warm from milking. The cream was skimmed with a shallow metal "dish" perforated to allow the milk to drain off. During the winter, the cream was kept in a fairly warm atmosphere, but during the summer it was essential to store it in the coolest place possible, perhaps outside, under a running tap.

Before butter making, the churn was scalded with boiling water and then cooled with cold water. The butter usually "came" after about 20 minutes of turning the handle, to make the beaters rotate. In the summer, the cream often "went to sleep" making a "slip-slop" sort of noise. This was a most annoying situation and slowed down the operation. When the beaten cream became a lump of butter, it was removed to a wet board on the draining board of the sink. It was then worked by hand to remove the butter-milk, after which it was either shaped into neat rectangles or pressed on to a "cow pat" and removed by blowing into the hole in the handle. The resulting pat was a neat round shape with a cow impressed on the top.

My parents decided I should go to the Dairy School in Gloucester, situated off Westgate Street, near the prison – no longer there. Miss Collet ran the school with the able assistance of Lilla Smith. Butter making was very different there.

At the Dairy School, cheese making took up most of our time. Milk for cheese making was brought to the dairy the night before and placed in large "jacket" vats – the temperature of the water inside the vat linings could be raised or lowered – rennet was added to the milk to make it "set", also anatto colouring. How much depended upon which cheese we were making, for instance the Cheshire cheese required more colour than single Gloucester, and Caerphilly none at all. By the morning, the cheese had turned to junket and needed to be cut into small squares. Gradually the curd was heated until the correct temperature was reached. The curd was tested by holding a chunk of curd against a hot iron strip, when it was withdrawn the threads had to be the correct length for the cheese which we were making. The curd was placed in moulds and these were then subjected to the correct pressure in a cheese press. After the press came bandaging, with muslin, before these 56 pounders

Trying out the dairy delivery bicycle, 1933.

were placed on shelves to mature – being turned, upside down, each day. The whey was drawn off and kept for the farmer to feed to his pigs.

Butter making and cheese making still continue today, in my friends' and relations' farmhouses, chiefly in the Severn Vale, but in a small way, because it is very hard work and time consuming.'

THE FOREST OF DEAN MINERS

The hard world of the mines was the livelihood of generations of Forest of Dean men.

DIGGING FOR A LIVING

'Born at the Dilke Memorial Hospital within the Hundred of St Briavels, a qualification that could have given me the right to be a Freeminer but for the fact that I will never work for a year and a day in a Forest mine, I grew up in the 1950s at what could be described as the tail end of the mining era in the Forest of Dean; the Cinderford valley where I live formed the East Mineral Basin of the Forest of Dean coal field.

The area at that time was remote from the rest of the county and somewhat insular. Iron and coal mining has taken place here for hundreds of years, bringing in people of a different character.

As a child you knew you were in the company of strong men. The hands that held your hand were calloused and chipped, and my father's face, like the faces of all the men in our district, carried the distinctive blue scars of deep and distant wounds laced with coal dust.

The miners of the Forest of Dean were men of strong character, hard working, somehow fierce but compassionate men, with a strong sense of humour. Most of them not only worked hard but played hard. Rugby and boxing were their sports – hard drinking men.

They were paid the little money they earned under what was

known as the butty system. The place or stall was registered in the name of a head collier or buttyman and it was he who was paid the wages by the Company. He was responsible for sharing or dividing up what money he thought fit with his butties, "the men who worked for him". This was often done in the pub after work before going home; the poor wife and children in some cases had to put up with what was left after a drinking session.

Work in the Forest coal field was very hard, because of its geology. The terrain underground was like that of the surface – hills and valleys, which did not lend itself easily to mechanisation. Boys at twelve years of age were treated little better than animals, having to put on the dreaded hod strap – a leather harness that bit deep into the shoulders, travelling down between the legs and attached by a chain to a box made of wood with wooden runners like a snow sleigh. This was how the coal was dragged out to the main roads underground – each young child, because that's all they were, dragging this box full of coal 30 or 40 yards, crawling along on hands and knees with their backs scraping against the roof of the workings. This is what I escaped from, thank the Lord.

My wife's grandfather was a miner, her great grandfather was a paper hanger from Pittville, Cheltenham. He came to the Forest like so many to find work in the mines. It was said that at one

The Speech House
Forest of Dean

time the population of Cinderford was mostly male and under 30 years of age. The town's market and shops stayed open until eleven o'clock on a Saturday night, the market being lit by naphtha flares. Cinderford was a sort of trading post for the miners; it once had 39 public houses.

Looking back to my childhood days, one thing that stands out in my mind was the sound of the pit hooter. I remember standing outside our front door in Valley Road, Cinderford on each New Year's Eve listening to the church bells and the pit hooters sounding in the New Year – you could tell each pit by the direction and sound of their hooters. The Northern United pit was loud and very near Cannop Colliery, a different direction. The Waterloo Colliery, Lydbrook came from the same direction as Northern United Colliery but much fainter in sound. It gave me, as a child, a very safe and warm feeling knowing that many miners were at work in our district, that they somehow would protect us from all dangers.

The colliery hooter had a very different meaning to the miners, for in the bad times, and there had been many, the sound of this hooter meant no work and no money to feed us.

After the Second World War, as pumping costs and underground distances increased, the coalfield became less economic – in 1965 the last big pit closed. Since then in many respects the mining scene has reverted to earlier days, with Freeminers on a small scale still exerting their long established rights.'

No More Freeminers?

'Trafalgar, New Fancy, Deep Navigation, Rose in Hand, Poolway Level, Success, Endeavour and Birch Hill Folly were some of the mines in the Forest of Dean. The seams of coal were often thin – less than two feet thick – and the work was hard. The collier was forced to lie at full stretch to cut the coal with his mattock and to use his shovel. Lighting was by candle. It was safest, as if the candle went out the air was bad. Another method of detecting bad air was to take canaries in cages into the pit. They would collapse if conditions were bad and work stopped. There was always the danger of roof falls and men often worked in wet conditions. It was a horrible job.

My father worked in the office at Camp Colliery from the age of 14. Thereafter he ran his own coal business and over the years became a Freeminer (born in the Forest of Dean and worked underground for a year and a day) although he never worked full-time underground. He complains that there will be no more Freeminers, due to there being so few home births, and with the closure of both Lydney and Dilke Memorial Hospitals for births, all babies are delivered in GP hospitals out of the Forest boundaries.'

VILLAGE TRADES AND CRAFTS

Every village seemed to be self sufficient in the past, providing work for its residents which ranged from the village shopkeeper to the local basketmaker. Many young girls went into service, in those days when having a servant was as normal on the farm as at the "big house".

A SELF SUFFICIENT VILLAGE

'In the 1930s almost all the people in Chedworth were farm workers, building workers or in the service of those two. Those on the farms included carters, cowmen, hedge layers and thatchers. On the building would be masons, carpenters, plasterers, plumbers and roof slaters, plus of course many general labourers on both sides. Other trades in the village at this time included the blacksmith, hurdlemaker, shoemaker, wheelwright and waggon maker, gamekeeper, carriers, roadmen and railwaymen. Chedworth had a post office and several shops, including a butcher and two bakers. In fact, the village could be said to be self sufficient, from the midwife to the undertaker.'

'Until 1939 practically everyone at Leighterton worked on the land. Nearby villages were reached on foot and paths criss-crossed fields leading to surrounding farms. Changes came with the war when a munitions factory opened in Nailsworth, work was more remunerative and people began to leave farming. Thus farms left with few workers turned to machinery.

The one pub in the village was an important meeting place for men on their way home from work. The policeman was also very much part of the community, cycling around the village every day on his bicycle and admonishing wrongdoers with a "good telling off" – this ranged from riding two on a bicycle, to pinching apples, brawling outside the pub – or checking gun licenses.

Village trades included a blacksmith, carpenter, shoe repairer, cycle repairer – all operating from the cottages – and a garage which would repair anything mechanical.'

The Cale family of Quedgeley making hampers for Gloucester market in 1928.

Thatching and Basketmaking

'My grandfather thatched many of the cottages on the great landed estates within a 25 mile radius of his home. Traces of his work can still be seen on the roofs of cottages around Britain's longest village green at Frampton-on-Severn. He caught the horse-drawn bus outside and alighted at the Whitminster terminus, walking the rest of the way to start work. Many was the night he spent in the hay barn with only a bottle of scrumpy for company if he felt too tired to trek home after a long day on the roof. One contemporary record claimed him to be the oldest active thatcher in Gloucestershire when 84 in 1949.

When he married and winter gales and snow made it impossible to work outside, he looked for another string to his bow and he took up basketmaking. There was a ready source of raw material lining the banks of the Severn and withies cut from the river Frome were loaded into a punt and pulled ten miles up the Gloucester/Sharpness Canal.

My family have now been making baskets of one sort or another for three generations. At one time our products were needed in many trades and we made eel putchins for the fishermen, cunning kipes, lamprey pots, huge fruit baskets for farmers and colliers at both Sharpness and Gloucester docks and hampers for Gloucester market.'

'My grandfather was the basketmaker in Kilcot village. There were also wheelwrights, who amongst other things made wheelbarrows, ladders etc and did repairs. There were woodmen, charcoal burners, farmers and odd-job men, hedge layers and many other country craftsmen.'

Wood and Stone

'My father was a woodman during the winter, at the beginning of the century, and regardless of the weather the day started at 7 am. Together with about half a dozen men he would walk to Linton Wood to cut down the deciduous trees marked for that year, and coppice other trees. They would also cut out all scrub and small trees, making bean sticks, hurdles and such. During the summer months he was employed on the land hoeing mangolds and turnips, haymaking, cutting wheat by hand and stooking.

Gorsley Quarry provided most of the stone for the local roads. This would be carted from the quarry to the roadside, there to be broken into small pieces by the stone breakers. The stone would then be spread along the road, covered with soil, watered well and the steam roller would come and flatten it, thus making a firm surface – dusty in summer and muddy in winter. The quarries were working until the 1950s.'

'The men of Chipping Campden often walked miles to work – my grandfather was a stonemason and would walk to Stow on the Wold. He would also do work at Hidcote Gardens, building walls etc. The men carried their "grub" in a flail, a flat bag made of straw which was fastened on their backs, or it was tied in a red spotted handkerchief which was carried at the end of a stick. In each pack there was sure to be a good piece of home-cured bacon and home-baked bread, often called a "thumb piece". I suppose it was held between finger and thumb and bits were cut off with a penknife. There would also be a lump of bread pudding and a bottle of cold tea, or maybe a bottle of cider.'

ESTATE PEOPLE

'I started work in January 1920, four months before my 14th birthday, on a smallholding in Winchcombe. Neither of my two employers were successful gardeners, so in 1926 I went to work in the gardens of nearby Sudeley Castle. I was employed as a journeyman under the foreman, Frank Chivers. The single men lived in a bothy, while the married men lived in tied cottages. There were three men in my bothy. We lived in spartan conditions, sharing a paraffin stove and a cold water tap. On another estate that I worked on later, six men died in a bothy, poisoned by the fumes of the coke stove.

I was thought good at my job and worked on several estates in Gloucestershire and Surrey. Gardening work was in great demand in the 1920s. When appointed Head Gardener of Harefield Grove by Sir Francis Neutigate, there were over 500 applicants for the job. The good times for gardeners working on estates ended in the early 1930s when there was a financial crisis. Many wealthy families were affected and some estate owners dismissed as many as six gardeners as a result.

The Squire and his tenants and estate workers often had a

good relationship. The Squire valued a good worker and provided the man "knew his place" something like friendship grew between master and man. This was also true of the relationship between the women and the mistress of the house. My wife was a housemaid at Harefield Grove.

However, one gamekeeper, whose work was so highly prized that the Squire presented him with a gun, became over familiar and was instantly dismissed. The removal cart was ordered to his cottage that very day! I was on very good terms with Sir Francis who would often offer me a pipeful of tobacco from his pouch as we discussed the gardens. The Dent-Brocklehursts at Sudeley Castle were good to their staff, as well as noted benefactors to the townspeople of Winchcombe. For example they were prepared to pay for any special medical treatment when a valued servant became ill, if it were not available in the town.'

IN SERVICE

'There were two big houses employing local people – Boxwell Court and Lasborough Manor. I started my working life at Lasborough when I was 14 in the 1940s. I lived in and earned ten shillings per week and my mother received 6s 6d because she laundered my caps and aprons. I was allowed one half day off each week and one Sunday a month. Other indoor staff included a butler, a housemaid and two women who went in daily.

I was given one month's training by the butler's wife. My day began at 7 am when I had to blacklead and light the kitchen range in time to cook breakfast for the household. Then came lunch, none of the ingredients for which were bought – everything came from the estate. Afternoon tea always included scones and cakes and then dinner had to be cooked. The family were waited on "hand, foot and finger" and work was hard but I felt that it gave me a very good training. The lady of the house kept the key to the store cupboard and a record had to be kept of everything that was used. And everything was used – all left overs went into the stock pot and everything was bottled, preserved or jammed.'

'Our family, three brothers and myself, was comparatively small in those days. Most families in the 1930s were large and poor.

Father worked hard but we never went without. We always had shoes on our feet (from the village cobbler who sold new shoes and repaired shoes too).

I went into service on the common at St Briavels at a large house owned by one of the gentry. Others went to work on the land or in one of the village shops. My duties, working for two sisters and a brother as pantry maid, meant I was responsible for keeping the china clean and the fireplace. I wore a cap and apron for waiting on table and once was praised by the cook for surreptitiously removing a slug from the vegetables which she had overlooked. Praise indeed! I had to be in by 9 o'clock at night and shared a room with the housekeeper who ground her teeth in her sleep. I had a half day off on a Wednesday and half a day every other Sunday. We had a 7 am start and wore an apron over our own clothes. The old lady used to have her breakfast with us in the kitchen unless there were house guests.'

THE VILLAGE SHOP

'One of our village stores at Leonard Stanley prided itself on supplying a mouth-watering array of home-produced meats. At the back of his shop James Harris kept pigs and from time to time engaged the services of Mr Vasey to kill the animals. As a child I remember being struck particularly by seeing him proudly striding around the village in his blue and white apron, a formidable armoury of knives, skewers and hooks hanging from a large belt around his waist. One day when visiting a house in Frocester with my father, I came across another aspect of the craft. In the parlour the never-to-be-forgotten sight of pigs hanging up all around in suspended animation awaiting the table.

The village post office was kept by an elderly neighbour of ours and as time went by she became less able to do the job. Even in those early days the post office sent out auditors to check that everything was being attended to properly. With every passing year our dear neighbour got more and more muddled and on the day of the annual check got herself so worked up that when the poor inspector came she would go off into a faint and have to be revived. The cure, which I saw being administered on more than one occasion, was most effective. They burned old rags over her!'

'The house where I was born in 1925 stands next to the Wheatsheaf Hotel at West End, Northleach. The front room on the hotel side contained the shop and, as a customer, you entered at the front door into the passage, and immediately turned left to open a half-door to gain admission to the shop.

The shop that I knew sold sweets and tobacco, and plants and seeds in season. The seeds were sold not only in the shop, but on rounds of neighbouring Cotswold villages – Chedworth, Bibury and Aldsworth among others. The "travelling salesman" part of the business occurred as a natural extension of a haulage business between Cheltenham and Northleach, with horse and cart, during my grandfather's lifetime. I never knew my grandfather as he died in 1924, but by all accounts he was a man of settled principles, and an evangelical preacher of free-church persuasion. The horse which drew the cart around the countryside was an old war horse named Tommy. He was an animal of uncertain temper, who once bit my father when he went to feed him one morning in our small rented field above the chapel cemetery, whereupon my father also flew into a temper and kicked Tommy. After that there was a restrained respect between the two of them.

In my day, the travelling seed business around the villages was conducted by car. This vehicle was hired from, and driven by, Fred Tea who kept the garage towards the middle of Northleach, opposite to Aunt Emm's grocery shop. I well remember the large, square, shallow baskets in which Dad carried his packeted seeds, all carefully assembled in their different varieties, each packet painstakingly stamped and the seeds – obtained as usual from the wholesalers, Messrs Johnsons of Boston, Lincs – meticulously weighed in our kitchen on the scales. Dad was very fussy about his seeds and during the last war was not too pleased when he had to take some from overseas. He was also well known to quite a number of his customers who, answering his knock, would welcome him with, "Hello, Bert, come in". Dad would inch his way through the door with his large square basket and pick out the packets as they read out their seed lists to him.

The shop was open very early to cater for smokers on their way to work. I cannot remember closing time exactly, but it was probably around 6 pm or 7 pm when Dad had looked up and down the street and gauged the likelihood of further custom.

I was young, but I remember the days of the slump in the earlier part of the 1930s. On one occasion I remember Dad coming out of the shop and saying to Mother, "I've just had Mr X (a traveller) in from Cheltenham, and I couldn't take anything from him as we are so overstocked." They were both upset about it as they knew their travellers well, but trade was very bad for a long time, and I have heard Dad say that some were glad of even ten shillings worth of business.'

'As the oldest child of a family of seven, I spent my childhood in the village shop and post office at Coaley. Family life was ruled by the shop and its opening hours, which were 8.30 am to 6 pm with half-day closing on Wednesday. Everyday needs were catered for and when wartime rationing was imposed and it was necessary for everyone to register with one shop for the essential foodstuffs, most villagers gave us their custom.

Groceries came in bulk, and serving the customers involved a good deal of weighing and packing. Sides of bacon hung in a giant five foot high meat safe, to keep out blow-flies. This meat would be deftly boned-out by my father before being sliced on the bacon machine. His strength was essential for skinning the huge Cheddar cheeses which he stored in the cellar to ripen and mature. Vinegar was decanted from a cask into jugs and bottles brought by customers for refills.

Fruit and vegetables were, in general, not stocked as most villagers had a productive garden, and kept a few hens. However, oranges and bananas were always in demand although not always available in the war years. The wooden boxes in which oranges were packed could be turned into cupboards and shelving, with a little ingenuity, and the soft paper wrappers, which were removed to check that the fruit was sound, were used by the family as luxury toilet tissue – much better than the hard shiny rolls sold in the shop. Long coffin-like boxes held the hands of bananas – which I, like many children, had to wait until after the war to taste.

The haberdashery drawer housed linen-covered buttons on cards, pins and needles in paper rolls, hanks of darning wools, and large spools of elastic which were measured to lengths required on the brass rule let into the counter-top. Hair nets came in several shades on large circular cards and boot-laces, essential for the farm workers, were cut from a strip of leather which hung in the shop window like a giant fringe.

Medicinal potions commonly stocked included Andrew's liver salts, Epsom salts, milk of magnesia, Friar's Balsam, syrup of figs and gripe water, as well as aspirin, cough mixture and chilblain ointment.

Washday needs were few, bars of Sunlight soap, Reckitts blue bags for rinsing whites, and Robin starch for dipping the linen. Candles, matches, spills, pipe cleaners and black lead for grates were in constant demand, while glass chimneys and wicks for oil lamps, mantles for tilley lamps, methylated spirits for primus stoves and mousetraps were essential household requisites.

Grocery orders were delivered to the outlying hamlets every Friday and Saturday evening; accumulator batteries for wireless sets were collected each week from households and recharged, and paraffin was sold from a trailer hitched to the back of the delivery van.'

THE LAST VILLAGE BLACKSMITH

'My father Charles John Taylor came to Witcombe as a blacksmith and wheelwright around 1896/97, settling in at the forge with his wife and family. The three storey house (now known as Clovelly) stood high up on a bank but the forge itself was at road level. The forge was divided into two sections, one half was for stabling the horses or for shoeing in bad weather and the other was the smithy or workshop. In one corner of this was the fire with its bellows and large wooden handle. All the tools were set out within easy reach and the anvil fairly central but nearer to the door, good light being essential. At times he had apprentices to whom he taught the trade, but often as his children grew older they were given the task of working the bellows.

The main road came past the forge at a lower level than the present one; it was known as the Old Drovers Road, a route direct from Fishguard to London via Birdlip Hill. On market days in Gloucester many a flock of sheep or herd of cattle were driven through. This brought passing trade as farmers drove carts or traps, where a shoe was cast or a cart shaft snapped from the strain of coming down the hill. Also during the First World War mules were driven along this route on their way to France, a trek for the poor animals plus many stops for a shoe to be replaced. Other than this he catered mainly for the local people, shoeing children's ponies, hunters or cart horses and repairing farm machinery.

The real craftsman side of his trade was fashioning gates or the type of fire grates that stood in an open fireplace, plus trivets in iron or steel, all being made with precision and skill.

When the old offertory box in Witcombe church was vandalised he made a new one with iron ornamentation, also a new hymn board, both being made from an old piece of oak that had once been part of a pew (these are still in use in the church). The village used to have two village pumps, one beside the Round House, the other opposite Reservoir Lane. Constant use of these pumps often resulted in parts breaking and a desperate plea would go out to the blacksmith for urgent repair.

The wheelwright side of his business was carried out in a barn-like building behind the forge. The entrance to this was situated between the forge and the orchard wall of the farm next door. He at one time made coffins and acted as undertaker, his first funeral being at Bentham church. His hearse was a motor carriage which he had bought from Mrs Crewdson (a relation of the Hicks Beach family), the registration number being AD 2.

Some veterinary knowledge of horses was always useful. He kept a supply of liniment for sprains and strains, but it was at curing colic that he was an expert. Someone would be despatched to Gloucester to purchase certain ingredients which would be mixed together, then poured down the horse's throat (known as drenching). While this was going on the horse was kept walking around as it was essential to keep the animal on its feet.'

Other Ways We Made A Living

There were, of course, dozens of other ways we made a living in the past and these are just a few recollections of times past, from elver fishing on the river Wye to life at the tarworks.

DENTONS, THE FASHION STORE

'On leaving Gloucester Art School in 1946 I began work at Dentons, Gloucester's most exclusive fashion store, as an apprentice display assistant. A rather scary experience for a shy young art student.

I worked under the guidance of a tall, elegantly dressed gentleman called Roy Driver from whom I learned so much about retail display and presentation. Mr Driver was an expert. He could display with flair anything from a bottle of expensive perfume to an exquisite ball gown. On Thursdays (early closing) he would often appear in a beautiful tweed suit and highly polished brogues to enjoy an afternoon in the Cotswolds.

The sales ladies were so beautifully dressed it was easy to confuse them with their wealthy clientele. They would arrive early looking so smart and then change into business clothes and then change again at lunch time or at 5.30 pm. They all sold on commission so competition was fierce. It was not unusual to observe them attending to two customers – often flitting between changing rooms. Always polite, always smiling, with remarks like, "That dress is really you, madam!"

At that time, the New Inn belonged to the same company. I spent many hours decorating the lovely old ballroom for social functions, parties, weddings and dances and the wonderful fashion parades when the sales ladies would become fashion models for the three days and evenings. How they loved showing off the exciting ball gowns, fabulous furs and jewellery and exclusive lingerie.

The window displays were often the talk of the town as we changed from season to season. Those were the days when the town centre was a blaze of lights and each shop tried to outdo the other, which did much to set the tone of a town or city centre.'

ELVER FISHING ON THE WYE

'In my younger days I lived in the Wye Valley, in the village of Brockweir. The river Wye rose as a spring at Plynlimmon in Wales and continued down the valley, growing in size to Chepstow, but it is only tidal between Chepstow and Bigsweir. All the local people understood the river and its tides and respected the dangers connected with it.

Work wasn't easy to come by in the 1920s and early 1930s and wages were low, so many familes were glad of the chance of making extra money. One of these chances was elver fishing in the spring, for which no licence was needed.

From the end of March until early May you saw men heading for the river, carrying on their shoulders a queer shaped scoop, made of fine meshed netting called elver net, which was the most expensive part of their equipment. This was fixed on a long, strong wooden handle. They also had a bucket, a clean sack, and if it was nearing dusk, a lantern, which enabled them to see the elvers rising on the tide, and also attract them to the side of the river.

Elvers are young eels, and travel hundreds of miles from the Sargasso Sea before reaching the rivers of the Wye and Severn. They come up on the tide twice a day at approximately half an hour later each time.

Most of the men who fished had daytime jobs, so went to the river for the later tide, often after dark, hence the need of a lantern. The river banks were quite slippery from the higher tides so the men usually worked in pairs, one holding the lantern, the other watching for the catch to be attracted to the light to scoop them up, and tip them wriggling into the bucket. If the catch was heavy there would be a number of buckets full to be put in the sack.

It was quite a sight to see the lanterns bobbing about for a considerable distance, on the riverside in the dark.

These sacks of fish were then washed many times at local wells; one well known spot at Brockweir was "The Spout", a source of spring water which came down from the hills, there was no piped water to houses in those days. The last wash was at home in hot water and salt to rid the fish of slime, then they looked like silver worms.

The wives would press the elvers into flat cakes about the size of dinner plates, and they were wrapped in butter muslin until they were cool, then unwrapped and put into greaseproof paper to be sold. Some families bought from the same fishermen each year, others preferred to buy the elvers loose and wriggling, and would clean their own so that they could cook them loose in bacon fat. The ones sold in the pressed cakes would be cut into slices, dipped in beaten egg and breadcrumbs with home-cured bacon. Whichever way they were cooked, they were always considered a great delicacy.'

TIMBER ON MAY HILL

'Small timber from the woods hereabouts (birch and sycamore) was made into brush heads and handles. Trunks of trees, some 13 foot long, formed the highest pile of timber in the county and were often taken to coal pits in the Forest of Dean. The men earned 30 shillings a week and worked from 7 am until 5 pm and on Saturday 7 am to 1 pm. Young lads got 15 shillings and 30 shillings when they reached 21. The boss only gave them Easter Monday off if they attended church on Good Friday!

To eke out their pay, many of these men resorted to poaching using wires, ferrets and guns. They caught rabbits, pheasants and pigeons, even foxes whose pelts were valuable. Bob Hook was an old inhabitant of May Hill, living in the house where he was born and where his father and grandfather were also born. A grocer and smallholder with milking cows, Bob quoted the Squire, Major Ackers, as saying the men in the area were "a nation of crofters" as besides working in the woods, on farms and at the brickworks, nearly all of them had a bit of ground to give them independence.'

MORELANDS MATCHES

'It was one big happy family at Morelands. We laughed and joked together and there was a great atmosphere amongst the girls. There were a lot of us and we certainly stopped everything on the Bristol Road when we left on our bikes. Fellows working in nearby factories called us "Sammy's Angels". Of course, there were bad days as with anything else.

Pay was not good and we worked on a bonus scheme. The rows and rows of machines started at 7 am. We worked from 7.30 am to 5 pm with an hour for dinner and a mid morning and mid afternoon break when we were able to have a fag. "England's Glory" were Samuel Moreland's best selling matches. The boxes had a ship on the front and jokes on the back. Our fingers bled from the sandpaper and I remember one girl took her engagement ring off so that it wasn't damaged. Somehow it got into a box and someone had a superb box of matches! My Dad made the red tips. There was a horrible smell in that part of the factory.

The factory produced 50 million matches a day. The timber came up the Berkeley Canal at one time. After debarking and cutting up, match size pieces were rotated on the machines and after the red tips were added, the match dropped into a box, lids were pushed on and finally sandpaper put on the side. Outworkers glued the boxes at home.'

THE TARWORKS

'The Tarworks, as it was known, was in fact a tar distilling factory. It was started by Wm Butler & Co Ltd of Bristol in 1860. Its function was to take crude oils from coal gas producers and treat it, producing pitch, tars, creosote, oils, naphthalene and other chemicals. The pitch was used in the building of boats, the tar for roads and creosote for wood preserving. In the 19th century, I.K. Brunel had pioneered its use in preserving railway sleepers.

During the Second World War, the tarworks was kept busy providing road tar for airfield runways. The tars and pitch were produced at Sandhurst, the many other by-products were processed at Bristol for use in industry and the chemical business.

The works were situated on the banks of the Severn at Sandhurst, opposite where the river splits through Maisemore to form Alney Island, about half a mile upstream from the Globe Inn. The factory received its raw materials by both road and river. Within the factory grounds were five cottages, built for employees and their families, in fact "tied cottages".

My father was such an employee, and just before the Second World War we moved into the largest of the five cottages. They were very basic, no gas, electricity or running water; these did not come until some time after the war. We never did have flush toilets.

Living there was an odd sort of experience; along one side of our garden were storage tanks, wells and vats, and along the other side was the river Severn. To get out to Sandhurst village or into town, we had to go either along the river bank and across the fields, or through the works, along its drive and out on to Sandhurst Lane.

There always seemed to be a barge or two moored outside the house, from which I could fish or swim – the river was not polluted then. There was always a flat bottom punt which I learned to handle before I could ride a bike. The punt was our means of transport during flood times when a boat across the fields was our only means of escape.

During the school holidays when I was considered old enough, I would travel with the various lorries to gas works to collect crude oils, or to stone quarries to deliver refined tar which was used in the making of tarmac. The trip that I most enjoyed was travelling up river to Worcester, to collect crude tar from the gas works there. It was a three day trip, starting early Monday morning and returning sometime on Wednesday, staying overnight at Worcester on Monday and at Tewkesbury on Tuesday. Sleeping on board a boat was something different!

The boats involved were a 50 ton capacity motor barge named *Jolly* built in 1903 at Appledore, towing a narrow boat named *Marie*. On reaching Worcester, the boats were moored to the quay wall on the Severn, the *Jolly* being too big to go into the basin leading to the canal which went all the way to Birmingham and other Midland places. The *Marie*, however, did get into the basin and was horse-drawn up the canal to the gas works to collect her cargo. She did this three times until both she and the *Jolly* were laden with crude tar, then the return journey began on Tuesday afternoon. As a lad it was a thrill to take the wheel of the *Jolly* during the trip and to lead the horse, which was hired from Worcester's Diglis basin, along the tow-path.

I finally left the Tarworks in 1958 when I first got married and moved to live in the city, which took some getting used to. Shortly afterwards my parents moved to a council house with all "mod cons" in the village. Father continued to be employed at the Tarworks until he retired. He had worked there for nearly 40 years, the last 30 as foreman.

As for the Tarworks, in 1952 Wm Butler formed The Bristol & West Tar Distillers, taking over other small producers of gas and tar. They in turn were taken over by The South Western Gas Co and then by British Steel, who closed it down in 1972.'

RULED BY THE HOOTERS

'Dursley was ruled by the hooters of the different factories. Four hooters went off between 6.50 and 7.30 am to ensure people got to work on time. Knapman Mill was one of the many mills in the area, and workers at Harolds Ropeworks were able to walk to work.'

BRIDGEND NURSERIES

'I was born in 1933 at Bridgend Nurseries, Stonehouse. My father was a nurseryman and seedsman and we owned three retail shops in Stonehouse – selling our own produce, mainly soft fruits and vegetables. There was also a florist side with cut flowers, wedding and funeral orders. There were no garden centres or pot plants in those days.

We had four and a half acres with seven greenhouses which specialised in chrysanthemums, with a few extras like orchids and freesias – until wartime restrictions prohibited fuel (coke) to heat the greenhouses being used for flowers only; so greenhouse production switched to tomatoes and cucumbers.

The florist side of the business was managed by my mother who, without any training at all, made magnificent wedding bouquets – arum lilies with fern which trailed to the floor. Mother made these wedding bouquets standing in front of a mirror, placing each large bloom correctly in the reflection. Wreaths were enormous affairs, very elaborate and costing, I believe, 1s 11d or 4s 11d. Fresh holly wreaths to be taken to the churchyard on Christmas morning were in fashion and my parents would stay up all night just before Christmas to complete all the orders. These wreaths would then be delivered by the errand boy on a bicycle – on Christmas Eve, or even on Christmas Day. Should it be a white Christmas, with roads too icy to ride the bicycle, the wreaths would be tied to a ladder which in turn was tied to the bicycle and the whole conveyance pushed along on foot.

Our first vehicle was an Austin Seven van – green with running boards and trafficators which sprang out at right-angles. My mother used this to distribute her produce to our three shops, deliver orders to Wycliffe College and to the local "gentry". Any surplus she then took to Gloucester market, bringing back other supplies such as potatoes and swedes – with me sitting on top of the sacks in the back of the van.

The next vehicle we had in the family was a large Morris

Oxford saloon which I learnt to drive in 1950. So big was it that my mother and I who were only five feet tall, had to have a false floor so that our feet reached the pedals, a built-up seat – and I still looked through the windscreen under the top of the steering wheel.'

THE BARBER

'My father was a barber and had served a three or four year apprenticeship, which was unusual in 1911. He had his shop in a room at the rear of a tobacconist's in the High Street, Tewkesbury, and the red and white striped barber's pole was placed high up on the front of the premises. He was always loved by children as he kept sweets for them if they were good when they had their hair cut. He also had the contract to shave and cut the hair of the inmates, as they were called, of the local workhouse.'

A HIGH CLASS GROCER

'I left school in 1928 and obtained a job with a high class grocer in town – shop assistant and book-keeper – which sounded very important. One soon comes down to earth, the hours were long and the work hard. By today's standards it was more like slavery but it was regarded as a way of life, and I just got on with it.

Provisions were delivered by wholesalers, in bulk; sugar, for example, in hundredweight sacks, which had to be weighed in one pounds and halves and stacked on shelves; likewise with soda which was used plentifully in the kitchens in those days. All cake fruits such as currants, raisins etc were delivered in small wooden rectangular boxes; these too were weighed which was a very sticky job. Tea arrived in big tea chests. Cheeses were huge and had to be skinned and portions weighed according to customers' requirements. Bacon was sliced with a cutter but this was not electric. Biscuits were not packeted but displayed in tins with glass lift-up lids.

When serving a customer the cost of items bought had to be totted up in one's head and the groceries packed in brown paper and tied with string into a neat parcel. We had a big outside trade, mostly monthly accounts, and it was left to me to send out the bills. We had a traveller who went out every day to collect orders and a delivery man to distribute the orders. When it was heard that someone new was moving into the district we delivered tea, butter, bacon and cheese and hoped to get a new customer. How different by today's standards!'

'In my very young days, the groceries from the Hughes' shop at Minchinhampton were delivered to the outlying properties, including Gatcombe Park, occupied by Col Ricardo, by horse and trap. I have vivid memories of the horse Jack, and I still possess one of his horse shoes.

My father told me that he used to deliver groceries, by horse and trap, to Coates, Rodmarton, Culkerton, Crudwell and Oaksey. These deliveries took him all day and he used to put up at night in the pub at Oaksey. On his return journey next day, he would call at the cottages, collecting their orders for delivery the following week. The orders, he told me, would always be for best butter, best bacon, best this, best that, never the cheapest.

The shop opened until 8 pm on Monday, Tuesday and Wednesday, 1 pm on Thursday, 9 pm on Friday and 10 pm on Saturday. A Mrs Garraway who lived in Butt Street, opposite the present police station, always arrived at the shop to do her week's shopping at five minutes to 10 pm on a Saturday, much to my father's dismay!

At the top of the yard of what is now Arden House, there was a building, now demolished, which was known as "The Bacon House". This building in my father's young days was used as a slaughterhouse for pigs, a job my father used to undertake – no stunning, no humane slaughtering, just a sharp knife and a slit throat. The bacon was cured in the same building and of course sold in the shop.

I remember the forge, opposite the post office, where Frank Smith used to repair the metal hoops we played with – whatever happened to hoop playing?

There was a Company grocers' shop called Walkers Stores in the High Street, run by the redoubtable Mrs Tombs and later by Miss Georgie Edmunds. The Hughes' shop and Walkers Store had an arrangement whereby one supplied the other with items in an emergency, and Mrs Tombs and my father would get together on a Saturday evening and work out who owed whom.'

The Hughes' shop at Minchinhampton.

NURSING AT CIRENCESTER

'I started my nursing career at Cirencester Memorial Hospital on 8th February 1948. I was 16 years old and too young to start training, which I did a year later.

The hospital had 60 beds, and consisted of a women's wards, a men's ward and a children's ward. All cases were treated together, ie medical, surgical etc. The wards were on the first floor as were the theatre and a small kitchen; on the ground floor were Matron's flat and office, staff dining room and kitchen, casualty, sisters' sitting room and bedrooms. In the attics were the sewing room and domestic staff bedrooms.

The nurses' home was the top floor of the building opposite, with the X-ray department, physiotherapy and pathology lab on the ground floor. The night staff slept in a cottage in Sheep Street, next to the hospital, part of which is now the Volunteer Bureau.

We worked split shifts, starting at 7.30 am until 8.30 pm with either a morning, afternoon or evening off duty plus one day off a week. We went on night duty for three months every year working seven nights on, three nights off. These were twelve hour shifts with an hour off sometime during the night. We gave

Charcoal burning.

complete care to the patients according to their needs.

The GPs performed all operations, each having their own specialities. We cleaned and sterilized all equipment and prepared all dressings for sterilization and also did most of the domestic cleaning.

There were sad times and happy times; people from my home village came in and some died. On one occasion I looked out of the window and saw a man shinning up the drainpipe (it turned out he was trying to see his girlfriend who was a maid), and another time a man burst in at the front door but on seeing me at the top of the stairs loaded with hot water bottles, ran away.

I had many happy times in Cirencester and left in 1951 to go to the Royal Hospital in Bath to complete my general training.'

THE CHARCOAL BURNER

'My father was a charcoal burner. Men worked in pairs – the work was long and arduous as it was essential to stay on the job.

The men lived rough as the fires needed constant attention.

Piles of wood were skilfully built up pyramid fashion, over six feet high with a centre opening. They were then covered with leaves, bracken and soil before the fire was lit. Four or five days later the heap was gradually reduced in size and then left for two to three days to cool.

The burnt logs were bagged up and taken by horse and cart to the local railway station for transportation to chemical works all over the country.'

Life and Work in Newent

'Horses in the streets – there was Jimmy Cooke with the baker's van with a little black horse wearing a muzzle because he used to bite the children when they offered him a sweet. He always knew the way better than Jimmy Cooke himself. If Jimmy stopped to talk to the ladies for too long when he was delivering the bread, the horse would wander on down the street and you would see old Jimmy Cooke coming out – he had a trilby hat and a long smock with a big baker's basket over his arm and shiny boots – and race down the street after the horse. This would happen day after day. He was a great character. He was also a postman and did one or two other jobs as well.

The Co-op had a baker's van – a bigger one and a bigger horse which used to graze in our orchard at the Market Square. Mr Parry was the driver. There was Guy Ford with his milk float who always whistled down the street – his favourite song being *Sweet Rosie O'Grady*. When his son used to help him and I was a small child, I remember looking out through the window to hear him shout, "Come on, get up lazybones."

I can see John Garlick now, he had a very fast trotting horse that used to fly up towards Newent and you could see him standing balancing towards the back holding the reins, his smock flying out in the breeze. Most of the farmers used to wear a smock – we call them warehouse coats now but these days they are much shorter. Of course, they were made from cotton then and were almost as good as a raincoat.

Whole families got their living from Lancasters sawmills. Several families from the cottages on the high pavement which has now been demolished used to work at the sawmill. One very vivid memory is that all the families who worked at Lancasters

Gloucester Docks.

had trucks for their firewood blocks – a perk from the company as they all had open fires in the cottages. The trucks had small iron wheels, a box for the wood and two shafts for the man to get in between. They pushed the empty trucks up in the mornings and all took their own bait (dinner time food). It was quite a long way from Gloucester Street to the Ross Road to the sawmills and the men would load their trucks with offcuts sometime during the day and when the hooter went at the end of the day, the men and trucks came pouring out of the front gates and off down the road.

Gathering speed, some of the younger chaps would take their feet off the ground, get their trucks to balance and ride down just on their arms, occasionally touching their feet against the ground to keep the thing from running away. They could always let the arms up and the shafts at the back end of the truck acted as a brake. It is hard to imagine these trucks going up and down every day collecting wood for their families. I remember the Mace family worked up there together with other families including the Dees. Old Mr Mace was coming down with his load of wood and Mrs Mace knew exactly when he would be down at the corner by the Market House. She would be there in her pinny and would run to the back of the truck and push him all the way up. Mrs Mace had the job of keeping the phone box by the Market House clean. She used to go off down with her brush and her duster and kept it spotless. After her time, the old phone box used to be in a terrible mess.'

WAR & PEACE

THE GREAT WAR 1914-1918

Though the war was fought far away, its effects were felt even in rural Gloucestershire – tragically so as the dreaded telegrams began to be delivered to homes across the county.

MEMORIES OF CHELTENHAM

'"One day we will have to fight the Germans," was one of my mother's sayings but she did not add that we would have to learn to hate them too. This was taken to extremes; people threw stones at innocent Dachshund dogs and if anyone had the misfortune to have a German-sounding name, it was quickly changed.

This was just a phase; before long the seriousness of war was established. Cheltenham then had six railway stations and was an ideal centre for organising troops, especially the London and South Western terminus which had a direct line to the South Coast. Empty houses were requisitioned to accommodate them; the "last post" always reminds me of the next door house at bedtime.

Volunteering was the order of the day; young men not in uniform were given white feathers by earnest young women. Cheltenham College had always had an outstanding "military side" and many people settled in Cheltenham to take advantage of this. As the casualties on the Western Front increased the sight of stricken wives and mothers became almost commonplace. Army notification was by telegram, a ring at the door and the sight of the telegram boy was the most dreaded event. It was usual to wear a black arm-band for the loss of a close relative. So often these were Second Lieutenants; they wore a distinctive diagonal shoulder strap easily recognised by the enemy when an officer led his men "over the top". Casualties were especially heavy in the 5th Gloucesters to which many Cheltenham men belonged.

Shortly before the war we had a children's party; all the "big boys" who came were killed in the next few years. Before the war ended no young men considered what career or profession they would like to aim at should they survive. Soldiers on leave never mentioned the horrors of the trenches, but once a chaplain on leave came to supper and said the duty he most hated was to be present when a man, mentally disturbed, was brought out and shot for "cowardice".

As time went on more and more hospitals were needed. Red Cross hospitals were manned by women who otherwise might have gone out to India to find an English husband. The number of these hospitals in Cheltenham was immense and all the staff became expert bandagers. It was long before the era of antibiotics. Wounded soldiers wore a blue uniform and were not allowed to stray. At the hospital next door to us a staging was erected to enable patients to view (and chaff) passersby.

Another feature was the lack of communications (no broadcasting then). Rumours were rife – an Angel of Mons and Strange Russians were said to appear. Only the *Echo* and daily papers had news. The *Echo*, then costing a halfpenny, issued special editions when necessary. I remember (my room being next to the street) coming down to breakfast saying that the newsboy was calling out a "great victory". But when I returned to lunch my mother said it was no victory – it proved to be the Somme.

Food was very difficult; what rationing there was fell very short compared to that in the Second World War. The "standard loaf" was very sour and once we tried the horse-meat available at the kennels. My mother, who must have been a favourite, said a shopkeeper had mouthed the word "cheese" to her – not about to take a photograph, but would she like a little bit? Butter was replaced by margarine and my father abandoned his nightly tipple in imitation of the King.

Songs were a wartime feature. They started with the jaunty *Tipperary* but gradually became sadder. Once we went on a cycling holiday; first stop Bristol where we stayed at the then popular (and cheap) Temperance Hotel. It adjoined a park where a woman came and sat on a bench and sang *Keep the home fires burning*. It was the saddest thing I'd ever heard.

Armistice Day was not celebrated extravagantly in Cheltenham; everyone seemed exhausted – we just had a fancy dress dance at our school.

Not long after, we heard that there were 5,000 "surplus women" in the country. Although there were then more jobs for women we were charged with stealing jobs from the men. Soon, however, women got the vote not solely, as is now often claimed, as a result of the Suffragettes' activities but because of their splendid war work.'

For Half a Pound of Butter

'As there was only one bus a week to Gloucester from Quedgeley, my mother walked five miles to the town during the war for half a pound of butter, only to find the shop closed when it was her turn in the queue.'

The Glad News

'It was a quiet morning on 11th November in the riverside hamlet of Etloe. Suddenly there was a great surge of noise as all the ships in the port of Sharpness blew blasts on their hooters. I was five and Eva from next door came bustling round. "The war is over, let's tell them in Blakeney." There were very few wirelesses then and no televisions, so we hurried to Blakeney and went to the Revd Allen. He went straight to the church and rang the bell joyously. Thus Blakeney heard the glad news.'

The Second World War 1939-1945

Once again we were at war, and this time civilians found themselves on the front line as German bombers brought the war to us. Some towns and villages changed almost beyond recognition as airfields were built close by and American and English servicemen moved in. Still, ordinary life went on.

Dogfight Over the Common

'A dogfight over Minchinhampton common between English and German pilots resulted in both being killed. The German is buried in the churchyard at Brimscombe.'

On May Hill

'Gloucestershire War Agricultural Committee decreed that much of the grassland of the county, except that needed for cattle, should be ploughed up. This included May Hill which was covered with bracken with some clumps of heather. The crops planted included potatoes but the whole idea was a washout. They broke more machinery with the shallow stoney soil than the effort was worth. Most of the hill has now reverted to bracken and gorse and is kept under control by the National Trust.

A group of German prisoners of war worked on the hill in the saw mills. First of all, they were transported to and fro from Highnam, then they camped in a small building at the mill. They used to love visiting the local homes, sometimes helping with the chores such as gathering in the wood and pumping up water from the well.

A number of Norwegian sailors got stranded in Gloucestershire on a whaling boat when war broke out. They came to lodge on May Hill and camped in the village hall. They helped with the timber felling in the woods. There is a large yew tree in the front garden of Glasshouse Villa, opposite the Glasshouse pub. This was originally fashioned by one of these Norwegians.'

Down Ampney Airfield

'The Second World War brought sights and sounds to the villagers of Down Ampney unimagined by our forebears. An area to the south of the village was surveyed and selected as suitable for an airfield. Construction began in 1943 and by the spring of 1944 Royal Air Force Down Ampney was a fully-fledged operational transport airfield with three runways. The complex network of hardstandings and dispersals, hangars, huts and miles of concrete roads became home to some 2,500 service personnel. Nearly 300 were WAAFs. The airfield was the base of Nos 48 and 271 Squadrons and housed 60 or so Dakota aircraft which brought back to the UK from the continent more than 20,000 wounded men, many initially to the 1,000 bed hospital specially constructed nearby.

Among the many gallant colleagues flying at that time from Down Ampney was Flight Lieutenant Jimmy Edwards, that man with the handlebar moustache who later gave comic performances as a showbusiness personality nationwide.

The RAF left in 1945 and the airfield closed in 1946. The beautiful stained glass window in All Saints church is dedicated to the men and women who took part in operations from here in 1944/45.'

BOMBS AND GLIDERS

'The night Woodmancote was bombed a stick of bombs fell across the village. The last one fell in Gotherington on a cottage in Shutter Lane, killing the occupants. Thankfully no one was hurt in Woodmancote. The bomb that fell in the garden of Kerrs Hill failed to explode. It sank in the clay and has never been found.

One night a crippled returning bomber of ours failed to clear Cleeve Hill. After passing over the village it crashed into the front of the hill, to the right of the gorse and to the left of the Rising Sun. I believe the rear gunner was the sole survivor.

In 1940 there was a threat of invasion and the Government placed emergency food stores throughout the country. The local food store was in the vestry at the chapel in Stockwell Lane. Church bells were also silent and were to be rung only as a warning of invasion.

Also in 1940 floods were high at Tewkesbury and Gloucester; it was very cold, so that the water froze. One night it rained and froze at the same time, and in the morning there were long icicles everywhere; telephone wires were down, telephone posts snapped off, birds were even found frozen to the trees.

There were few interruptions to school attendance. The grammar school and the technical school pupils had some days off after the night of the worst raid on Cheltenham when the railway line was closed because of an unexploded bomb. At other times 13 and 14 year olds went from school to pick up potatoes in the fields. Pay was 6d per hour.

In the later war years the sky over the village was full of the constant drone of towing aircraft, releasing their gliders overhead, whence they glided back to base at the Stoke Orchard airfield, a training school for glider pilots.'

PREPARING GLOUCESTER CATHEDRAL

'On the outbreak of war in September 1939 the cathedral became an important vantage point used by firewatchers. These were unpaid volunteers, both women and men, who patrolled the roofs of the cathedral by night anxious to spot any incendiary devices dropped by the German Luftwaffe. The Dean, Dr Harold Costley-White, was regularly on duty with them.

There were naturally great fears for the security of the cathedral and its treasures in the event of a Nazi air attack. It was thought that Gloucester with its aircraft industry and railway works might be an important target.

By February 1940 all the precious glass had been removed from the great east window and the openings boarded up. Every panel was carefully packed and labelled. Half of it was taken to Miserden Park, about eight miles from Gloucester, and stored in the wine cellars which were specially strengthened for the purpose. The remaining panels were deposited in the cathedral crypt.

Many other treasures were bricked up in the crypt for the duration of the war. The most important was the Coronation Chair sent from Westminster Abbey in 1939 in a wooden case, the contents of which were a mystery to all but a few. Items from Gloucester Cathedral included the effigy of Duke Robert of Normandy and the Lady Chapel's Annunciation window.

Other valuables were protected by sandbags. These included the tomb of Edward II and the Morley and Blackleech monuments. The Prinknash glass in the south walk of the cloisters was protected in the same way.

In the event of a German incendiary attack, many people believed that water from the firemen's hoses could have caused more damage than the actual bombs. Drainage holes were made in various places, including in the medieval fan vaulting of the cloisters, to prevent water settling in pockets.

Sadly, the cathedral did lose one of its treasures during the war. This was a 16th century altarpiece depicting the Last Judgement. Before the outbreak of hostilities, the painting was taken to London for restoration but the restorer's studio was totally destroyed by incendiaries in February 1944.'

GLOUCESTER CATHEDRAL

THURSDAY, MAY 10th, 1945, at 6.45 p.m.

RECITAL OF MUSIC

KATHLEEN FERRIER

(CONTRALTO)

HERBERT SUMSION

(ORGAN)

Under the auspices of

THE LADIES' COMMITTEE OF THE FRIENDS OF THE CATHEDRAL

PROGRAMME.

PRAYERS.

1. Passacaglia in E minor - - - - *Rheinberger*
2. "Prepare Thyself Zion" (Xmas Oratorio) / "Slumber beloved" - - - - / "Have mercy Lord on me" (St Matthew Passion) — *Bach*
3. Dithyramb - - - - - - *Harwood*
4. HYMN (E.H.) 471.

PRAISE to the Holiest in the height,
And in the depth be praise,
In all his words most wonderful,
Most sure in all his ways.

O loving wisdom of our God!
When all was sin and shame,
A second Adam to the fight
And to the rescue came.

O wisest love! that flesh and blood,
Which did in Adam fail,
Should strive afresh againt their foe,
Should strive and should prevail;

[OVER

A celebratory recital was held just after VE Day at Gloucester cathedral. The programme was signed by Kathleen Ferrier.

COLOUR BAR

'American soldiers, both black and white, were based at Ashchurch army camp near Tewkesbury but strict segregation was enforced. I remember a black soldier asking my mother if he could speak to my 18 month old blonde sister. Colour meant nothing to her. He said, "Excuse me, ma'am," when she smiled at him and saw him looking at her. He held my sister in his arms and spoke to her. At the time we didn't realise he had probably never held a white child. He gave my mother some chocolate for my sister and chewing gum for me and my friends. My mother's comments on the fact that black men could die for their country but had to stay segregated were not repeatable.'

SILVER ELEPHANTS!

'We had a barrage balloon deterrent around Brockworth to stop the German planes from bombing the aircraft factory where, amongst others, the Hurricane fighter was built. There were about 23 balloon sites all round the village and whenever the Germans came over, up they would all go – great silver elephants up in the sky! Unfortunately once or twice a balloon was hit and when it came down our electricity supply was cut off. This made the blackout easy to maintain!'

BUSES AND FILMS

'During the war there was an hourly bus service between Painswick and Gloucester. Very few people had petrol to run their private cars so these buses were very full. To make room for more passengers the seats on the buses were rearranged and put round the bus with their backs to the windows so that there was more room in the centre for standing. The journey to Gloucester was fairly normal, but when coming back to Painswick, it was advisable to join the queue for the bus about 30 minutes before it left to be sure of getting a place, maybe even a seat. Sometimes, for some unknown reason, the bus failed to appear and this meant a further hour's wait.

The buses were old and found Upton Hill very difficult. Near the top on its steepest part the buses would sometimes come to a grinding halt. First the men would get off, and if the bus still couldn't make it, the women would have to get off as well and

THE GUILDHALL, GLOUCESTER
September 28th, 1944

CONCERT

IN AID OF CENTRAL FUND FOR REFUGEES

Programme

Sonata in G Minor .... *Marcello*
WOLFGANG BRETSCHNEIDER—'Cello
RICHARD GLAS—Piano

"Where'er you walk" .... *Handel*
"Gretchen at the Spinning Wheel" .... *Schubert*
"The Trout" .... *Schubert*
MARIA GOLDBERG—Mezzo-Soprano
EVA MANES—Piano

Andante and Variations in B♭ Major .... *Schubert*
RICHARD GLAS—Piano

INTERVAL

Trio in D Minor .... *Mendelssohn*
RICHARD GLAS—Piano
RONALD BOWLES—Violin
WOLFGANG BRETSCHNEIDER—'Cello

"Melodious Strains of Gladness" .... *Brahms*
"Eternal Love" .... *Brahms*
MARIA GOLDBERG—Mezzo-Soprano
EVA MANES—Piano

Study in E Major .... *Chopin*
Scherzo in C Sharp Minor .... *Chopin*
RICHARD GLAS—Piano

NOTE.—The songs, with the exception of the first, will be sung in German, the English translation of which will be found on the back of this programme.

A concert in aid of refugees held at Gloucester, much of it sung in German!

walk up the pitch behind the bus. On one occasion we all had to push the bus up the last lap of the hill. When we finally arrived at the top of the hill and started to come down into Painswick through the Plantations some drivers, no doubt hoping to save petrol, would turn off the engine and free wheel. The bus would hurtle down Gloucester Road and Gloucester Street, no one-way system then, and come to a grinding halt at the crossroads. This so frightened me that I would ring the bell halfway down, stop the bus, and walk home.

It was almost impossible during the war to obtain film for a camera. All available film was used for aerial photography. We had a very enterprising chemist in our village who turned his attic into a dark room and made up films with old spools, old backing papers and Patchomatic film which could be bought from the Air Ministry in sealed tins, this being offcuts from aerial film. He and a friend devised a method of cutting this film to fit the old spools and backing papers. The film was taken from the sealed tin, laid on a board over which a frame was placed. A cutter ran along the edges of the frame cutting the film to the exact size required. This piece of film was then attached to the backing paper, wrapped around the spool and secured. All this had to be done in complete darkness and without touching the surface of the film. It took me quite a while to get into the way of doing it. One of the problems was that the film had been rolled tightly in its tin, and when cut, if not controlled would roll itself up again and escape across the table on to the floor. I was paid 6d for each completed film!'

GOOD USE FOR A GAS MASK

'My father, the village milkman at Coaley during the war, came across an amusing sight one day on his travels. An author, who was very tall, and his wife, who was very short, had taken a cottage in the village and eventually it became necessary for them to dispose of the waste from the "little house" at the bottom of the garden. They had prepared a hole in the garden and when my father saw them, had donned their gas masks and were carrying the smelly receptacle between them, somewhat lop-sidedly. A very enterprising couple.'

SHORTAGES

'Working in an office at Dowty, a bride to be was threatened with prosecution if she left without permission as she was doing war work. She took a chance and many anxious months and even years followed, though nothing came of it. Because there were so many girls getting married to their servicemen sweethearts the collection for wedding presents had to be stopped in the office. One girl was sold a very special tin of luncheon meat for her wedding reception, special because it was the only meat which could be bought at that time and the grocer had managed to reserve one or two wholesale-sized tins.

At some public houses in Cheltenham it was known for people to go early on purpose to secure a glass, which they held onto all evening – due to short supply there would not be enough to go round. On the railway stations the WRVS frequently served tea in jam jars because of the shortage of cups.'

GUARDING THE COUPONS

'My parents kept a general stores in Dursley during the war. I remember the small pieces of paper all over the dining room table at the end of each month. These were the coupons cut from the customers' ration books and all had to be counted by us and woe betide anyone who sneezed or banged a door and caused any coupons to go on the floor. The coupons were smaller than a present day postage stamp and were put in different envelopes for tea, sugar, butter, bacon, cheese and so on. The following day it was my duty after school to take the sealed envelopes to the local Food Office at Kingshill House. Never were envelopes so closely guarded, as we depended on the number of coupons submitted for our permits for future supplies. The cutting and weighing of rationed items was a very skilful affair as very little waste was allowed for on our permits.

The day bananas arrived was a red letter day for some but a headache for the retailer in deciding who could have the "golden treasures".'

We Did Our Bit

Everyone did their bit for the war effort, whether it was fund raising, serving in the Home Guard or the Women's Land Army, or working at the aircraft factory or the post office —just some of the memories of those on the Home Front.

Fund Raising

'During the war my mother served on a village committee organising various functions to raise money to send Christmas gifts to our serving men and women in the Forces.

One of the functions was a pantomime, *Sleeping Beauty*, scraping together what talent could be found to put on the show. It proved to be a success and was well received. One of the cast – the leading light – was a lady evacuee who had been a professional on the London stage, and with her expertise and encouragement a regular revue company "The Broadwell Revellers" was formed, putting on two shows a year for several years.

There were four men in the company, five ladies and two girls (we were about 13 years of age at the time) as well as a girl pianist, electrician and back stage helpers. As well as being a professional singer and dancer the lady was also an accomplished dressmaker who made all our basic costumes of blackout material and white butter muslin – neither of which were on ration – and others of coloured crepe paper, apart from what was borrowed or begged from friends and neighbours.

The programmes consisted of songs, sketches and monologues

and as they improved so our fame spread abroad and invitations came to go "on tour" to neighbouring villages. The first of these was a request to do a performance at a nearby village the other side of the hill.

Petrol rationing was in force and in order to be patriotic, the decision was taken to transport people, props and costumes using a flat bed trolley with temporary sides, withy poles and rick sheeting to make a type of covered waggon drawn by two heavy horses – one in the shafts and one in front.

All went well with the show and afterwards the cast were well rewarded with food and plenty to drink. Setting off for home the adults chose to walk the steep part of the hill to lighten the load. Children were allowed to ride and it was my task to do the driving as I was familiar with horses.

It was a dark night. Blackout was in force everywhere and as we approached the top of the hill – a junction with the main road – a voice called out loudly, "Halt, who goes there?" We were taken aback but giggled nervously and the horses plodded on. Again the voice agitatedly shouted, "Halt again, I say halt."

Then one of the elders from behind, realising that it was the local special constable, said calmly, "What's the matter, George – did you think it was the b..... Germans?"'

'A committee was formed at Fairford to collect for Navy Week. Somebody had the idea to build a submarine and float it on the river at the Town Bridge. Artie Golding, a carpenter, was asked if he could build a submarine. The answer must have been yes as in due course the submarine was launched on the river. Now, we had a wonderful character in Fairford by the name of Bertie Wayne – he was only five foot four inches tall and always wore a bowler hat, a frock coat, black trousers and boots. Add to this a grey beard, bandy legs and that when you talked to him it was very difficult to understand what he said; to complete the picture he rode a tricycle. So somebody was needed to be on the deck of the submarine for the launch. Who? Well now, Bertie was about the right size and he would love to get dressed up and stand on the deck and have his photograph taken, if anybody had any film. The great day arrived, the start of Navy Week. Bertie was dressed in a sort of admiral's uniform – it left a bit to the imagination. From the steps in Busbys garage forecourt, Bertie stepped onto the submarine, the folks watching on the bridge all cheered then, to our amazement, the submarine slowly began to sink. Poor Bertie got very wet!'

At the Aircraft Factory

'I was conscripted for war work in 1942. After a brief training in the use of hacksaw, file and drill, I was classed as a semi-skilled fitter and sent to work for the Gloster Aircraft Company. My first post was at a dispersal factory which occupied half the bus depot in London Road, Gloucester. Here we made wings for Typhoon fighter planes. Soon the section moved to a garage in Worcester Street.

Then we found out that we were going to a purpose-built factory at Newent. Working there entailed getting up at 5 am, catching a works bus to the station, then travelling by train to Newent and finally walking up a lane – to start work at 7 am. The walk was very chilly at that time of day. Eating breakfast so early meant that I was always ready for the thick slabs of buttered toast that were brought round the factory in the morning. Although the days were long the work was varied and *Music while you work* helped the time to pass quickly.

After about nine months out at Newent, we heard the welcome news that the section was moving back to the bus depot in Gloucester. This was much handier for the shops, and an early pass at 5.15 pm once a week meant we could go to the pictures.

I stayed there until the section disbanded, shortly before the end of the war. Then I transferred to Brockworth, to work on the Meteor. This involved my first experience of working night shifts but fortunately the end of the war soon put a stop to that.'

'As a teenager in St Briavels before the Second World War, there was very little other than domestic service in the way of work. That is why I found myself living in lodgings in Tivoli Road, Cheltenham and working at the Aircraft factory, following a spell in service at the age of 14.

The work itself was very boring, working on copper and aluminium pipes. It was tedious deburring with emery paper those bits which went to make up the planes. I still bear the scars in the way of varicose veins from banging down the foot pedal on the riveting machine.

We worked on a shift system from 6.30 am to 5.30 pm when on days. The company employed around 300 men and 80 to 90 women and my education was completed in all respects, although there was never any hanky-panky from the married men. They also looked suitably ashamed if they thought you had overheard them if they swore. We women waited on the men and fetched their break-time tea from a big urn brought around the departments. However, it gave us the opportunity to sort out the most gooey dripping cakes and reserve these for ourselves. These were brought in daily from Ferris' the Bakers together with doughnuts and chelsea buns. We could also purchase a bread roll for 1d, spread for a halfpenny, and a piece of cheese for 2d for our lunch. We paid 30 shillings a week for our lodgings and five shillings bus fare. We were attired in "bib and braces" at first then moved on to green overalls – very fetching.'

'Early in 1941 as a young man of 18 years, I was with some others who had been called in to work at the Gloster Aircraft Company, building new hangars on No 3 site. One day four of us were working at the far end of the factory when the lunchtime whistle blew. We moved round and sat on some scaffolding facing the airfield. Unusually, nobody else seemed to be about – unknown to us all the regular workforce had been sent away from the airfield (to a free meal in the canteen, I believe).

As we were eating our sandwiches, a small aeroplane came out of a hangar and taxied up the airfield. We noticed that it had no propeller. It turned, taxied back, turned again and stopped. Then it taxied up the airfield again, much faster this time. Halfway along the runway it left the ground, rose about four feet in the air, flew for a short distance, then landed, went to the end of the runway, turned and taxied back into the hangar.

That night when I told my father that I had seen an aeroplane flying without a propeller, he said, "You must have been dreaming, lad."

It was not until 1945 when I was home again, on leave from the army, that we realised that I had unwittingly witnessed the first flight of a jet-propelled aircraft!'

'Aircraft Components of Cheltenham was a small company founded by George Dowty, once an employee of the Gloster Aircraft Company, who had realised the need for the specialist manufacture of aircraft equipment. At the beginning of the war, the company was already involved in design and manufacture of many of the famous fighter and bomber aircraft.

The war inevitably brought additional problems to industry. Because of the urgent need for arms and equipment, supplies to the armed forces had to be guaranteed, even in the event of air raids. Manufacturing supplies were duplicated or triplicated, and documents, drawings and all records duplicated or triplicated as a precaution against direct hits.

Direct hits were not a fantasy. Gloster Aircraft factory brought the area into a high risk zone, evidenced by the barrage balloon defences around the eastern side of Gloucester and the rows of dense smoke-producing oil drums set all along the country lanes of the Brockworth/Churchdown area to produce a thick layer of "fog" to blot out the targets from the air. Brockworth was a special target because of the GAC Armstrong Whitworth shadow factories producing the Albermarle Bomber and the first jet-propelled aircraft. Other defences included large anti-aircraft guns which fired every time aircraft flew overhead – at one stage a nightly occurrence, with the occasional daytime sortie. All this did not pass without an element of excitement at the age of 16.

Working hours for industry were long with a five and a half day week plus compulsory overtime and, for the school leavers, poor salaries. Sunday overtime brought me 1s 2d of which 1s 1d paid for lunch in the canteen. This after cycling from Newent to Cheltenham.

Petrol rationing plus a small salary increase brought along a touch of luxury – motorcycle transport. This made the mandatory technical college attendance in the evening more feasible. Journeys for pleasure were of course eventually banned and petrol coupons were issued by the authorised officer for essential journeys only.

The rapid development of the aircraft industry was a bonus to the Cheltenham-based company, subsequently named Dowty Equipment Limited and then the Dowty Group, which gradually diversified to cover the increased range of aircraft equipment. Landing gear, hydraulic systems and fuel systems took on their own specific roles and specialisation and identification as separate companies within the group.

Rarely was there the chance, however, to see the fruits of your labour in the form of a completed aircraft. Morale was raised by meagre lunch-time *Workers Playtime* variety shows in the canteen broadcast live to the country, *Music while you work* one hour each morning on the factory floor (not in the offices) and occasional VIP visits. One such visit was by the Duke of Kent, shortly before he was killed in action.

There was some sense of achievement and satisfaction to have participated in the design of landing gear and equipment for so many aircraft, without which the war may have ended very differently. From the early bombers such as the Bristol Beaufort to the Lancaster, Halifax, Vulcan and the development of fighters which won the Battle of Britain, to the faster jet aircraft and the in-between fighter bombers which combined to assist so strongly with the D-Day landings, the part played by Dowtys was essential to the war effort.'

Posted to Gloucester

'As a 20 year old RAF pilot in early 1943 I was posted from Little Rissington to RAF Staverton, now Gloucester's civil airport. Having been born and bred in London and at school in Kent, the countryside of Gloucestershire was a wonderful place to be doing a wartime job which I enjoyed.

I flew the Avro Anson aircraft at the Staverton Navigation school, which involved training navigators, bomb-aimers and wireless operators who would go on to fly operations over Germany. We were often occupied in dropping practice bombs on Frampton sands in the Severn estuary in order to perfect the performance of the bomb-aimers for future more serious sorties.

After a few months at Staverton I was moved to the satellite airfield at Moreton Valence and from here most of the flying was done at night. These night details were designed to give practical navigation experience to aircrews and usually took about three and a half hours. Such trips included the Isle of Man, North Wales, Lincolnshire, Norfolk, the South West peninsula and Ireland, during which navigators were expected to guide the aircraft and return safely to base.

On some occasions navigators lost their way, became airsick, or fell asleep and it was then assumed that the pilot knew exactly where he was at all times, whether over 10/10th cloud or not, and that he would bring the aircraft safely home no matter what!'

IN THE POST OFFICE

'Fortunately, as a fully fledged PO clerk, I was in a reserved occupation from the start of the war.

Over the next six long years, when, sometimes, we thought the war would never end, all the 18 to 20 year old boys were taken, then those in their twenties and then those in their thirties, and the girls had to do more and more of the work until, eventually, we ran the sorting office, the telegraph room *and* the counter. Busy was hardly an adequate word – we never stopped. The shifts were long and the work hard. Manning the sorting office meant, for me, arriving at the back door on the dot of 6 am to find the large Gloucester mail van and two or three postmen who had just arrived to unload it. I had to cycle three miles whatever the weather. It was wonderful on fine summer mornings but not so pleasant on icy roads in winter-time. We worked until 2 pm when I cycled home and then returned at 4 pm to help until 7 pm with the sorting of the evening mail. The general atmosphere and the way in which all the postmen happily accepted being overseen by young girls, was wonderful. I thoroughly enjoyed my work and, off duty, was far too tired to worry overmuch about the war.

A succession of troops were billeted in the town. One didn't think too much of the fact that this was their last stop before France and the trenches. They were billeted in draughty old factories but their cheerfulness was amazing. The extra work they brought to us was phenomenal, but it was a point of honour to dispatch *everything* on hand in the sorting office in the mail van to the station at exactly 6.30 pm. There were two classes of mail – letter post and printed paper rate (unsealed). There rarely was anything left behind – and then only a few at printed paper rate. If the mail was heavier we just worked harder and quicker! Considering the worried state of our minds, and the tendency towards human error, it was extraordinary that almost everything arrived at its destination the next morning. The public were always assured their letters would do so – and they did.

For two or three days after the war started someone had to man the phone to take down the reams of instructions relayed to us. Wartime rules were quite a different kettle of fish to peacetime ones. Blacking out all the windows was a priority as we anticipated early air raids. As time went by telegrams abounded. As the telegraph boys had gone off duty long before the counter staff, I would volunteer to deliver a late telegram on my way home. Sometimes it was to inform relatives that a soldier, thought to have been lost in battle, was a prisoner of war. I rejoiced with the family. I was lucky not to have the job of delivering one saying "killed in action". Once there was quite a row when a father came along to complain of his daughter who had just had a baby, being handed a telegram to say her husband had been killed. Tragic – but what solution was there?

Work at the counter was quite overwhelming. Queues were the order of the day, often reaching out into the street. Soldiers billeted in the town wished to communicate with their relatives and those people with men in the forces used Airgraphs (about 15 inches by nine inches) with a small space for the address at the top and a larger one for the message to send abroad. They were handed out to the customers who handed them back when written. We sent them away to be photographed and a miniscule copy was sent on. (Soldiers abroad also used this means of communication.) We had "Save for Britain" and "Buy a Spitfire" weeks. Almost everything was rationed, on coupons, or unavailable, so there was nothing much on which to spend any spare money. People saved to help the war effort, chivvied on by a great deal of advertising. The more they saved the harder we were obliged to work.

To our surprise on opening the office doors one morning in 1940, we found a lot of ragged, unwashed, ill-dressed soldiers, most of them with no caps and an assortment of uniforms, on the doorstep. We soon found out that they'd been evacuated from Dunkirk. The wireless, as usual playing down the war, had told us of rearguard action so we had not really guessed the extent of this retreat. Over the telephone came streams of instructions telling us, for one thing, to change their French currency for English money. We were tremendously busy that day.'

Heavy Engineering

'Warwork brought me from my native Scotland in 1939 to a rented house in Rudford. I was employed by Fielding and Platt, the heavy engineering firm in Gloucester, down the Bristol Road. There was no petrol for the car so a few of us used to meet up at 7.30 in the morning and bike, whatever the weather, into town. We often worked until eight at night, and sometimes then changed into uniform and guarded the factory overnight. Fieldings produced machinery for guns and shells and huge cranes were overhead all day long.'

IN THE HOME GUARD

'I worked as a foundryman at RA Listers in Dursley at the outbreak of war. In June 1940 the situation was anything but funny; following the miracle of Dunkirk everyone thought that the invasion of Britain was almost a certainty.

An appeal was made in the newspapers and on the radio for every able-bodied man to volunteer to defend their country by joining what was then called the Local Defence Volunteers. I signed up and got involved in the Stonehouse force, which was run by former officers from the First World War from headquarters above a shop.

While we were all enthusiastic, we knew that we would be no match for the trained German paratroops and were very apprehensive and, while we didn't show it, extremely frightened.

As the war went on, the volunteers were reorganised, fitted with uniforms and renamed the Home Guard. At last we felt we were real soldiers and were immensely proud to wear regimental badges – our morale jumped by 1,000 per cent.

The Stonehouse platoon was ordered to provide a nightly guard on the LMS viaduct at Beards Mill and, later in the war, to guard Stanley Mill at Ryeford, which was used as a Royal Navy store. The platoon was also involved in manoeuvres with other Home Guard units in Woodchester Park and in a mock nighttime attack on the Sperry Gyroscope company at Bonds Mill. For the latter we were told to act as though we were German paratroopers seeking to capture and destroy the factory. After various scout reports and a wet attempt to attack the factory through a culvert carrying the river Frome under the railway line, the attack was called off as it was too well guarded. Sperry, because of the importance of the work to the war effort, had one of the largest Home Guard units in the area, with a Lewis gun mounted on top of the factory's security hut.'

'The much laughed at *Dad's Army* so aptly portrayed by Captain Mainwaring and his gang took many hours of our spare time with one evening a week and every Sunday morning as training sessions, plus the regular guard duty every six days.

The guard was mounted outside the Newent Home Guard headquarters from 9 pm until 6 am with three men taking shifts, standing outside with fixed bayonets in turns. It was difficult to stay awake then and continue the following day at work!

Duty and training were taken seriously and in spite of the old Local Defence Volunteers' image of fork and pike warfare, equipment more apt for serious defence became available: .303 rifles were available for everyone, Lewis machine guns, hand grenades, guns which fired three inch diameter bottles of flammable liquid capable of destroying tanks, and Sten guns became available for serious training and use if necessary. Even the Signal Section was issued with Aldis lamps for longer distant visual morse code, radio communication – a portable transmitter/receiver weighing 20lbs, and a 350 BSA motorcycle, for which I was grateful because it brought with it special duties.

The humour on which television's *Dad's Army* was based was so true to real situations and many a script could have been added from the Newent platoon.

For example, one evening during rifle loading practice, a trigger was accidentally pulled with the rifle loaded. No one was injured but the bullet went through the ceiling and ricocheted round the room above, circling a bed in which poor old Mrs Clark aged 80 was sleeping. She was unaware of the event!

One Sunday morning during matins, one of the Signals Section slipped while climbing over the church bells to reach the tower battlements, where communication was to be made by Aldis lamp with the Churcham platoon, on top of May Hill. The resultant slip made a loud ring on the church bell – the signal that Britain was being invaded!

The radios issued to the Signals Section had one bonus when training fell on a Thursday evening. Walking round country lanes, in different directions, members of the section could practise their communications, but at 8 pm the call went out, "ITMA over and out." This was the signal that Tommy Hanley's BBC programme *It's that man again* was on the air. Members of the Signals were unofficially privileged not to miss the best programme on the air.'

'The Home Guard on May Hill was attached to the Longhope platoon and headquarters was Longhope Manor. It was a motley crowd by all accounts and one of them said, "If the Germans *had* come, they would have killed the whole lot of us in five minutes!"

There was a fright once when everyone was told to stand by as the Germans had landed at Dursley. Everyone was both excited and frightened which soon turned to dismay and relief when they were subsequently informed that the Germans had landed at Guernsey and *not* Dursley!

The May Hill squad were all armed with shotguns and rifles and took turns to man the lookout post on May Hill. This consisted of a small hut situated in one of the small depressions on top of the hill. Four of them were on guard up there, two on active guard and two resting. They always carried up jars of cider to console themselves and help see the night through. It was noticed that the German pilots seemed to use the top of the hill as a landmark, the planes turning immediately above it on their way to bomb Gloucester, Cardiff and Coventry. Several bombs were dropped in the vicinity – two at Aston Ingham, one at Blaisdon railway bridge on the Gloucester/Longhope/South Wales line and there was an unexploded bomb at Taynton, which the army disposal team were called in to deal with on a Sunday afternoon.'

'Very early in the war, before I joined the regular army, I was a member of the Home Guard. We had been told one night that if the sirens sounded we were to report to Windmill Lodge on the edge of Minchinhampton common up Windmill Road. The sirens duly sounded at about 2 am. I fetched out my bicycle and tore up Windmill Road. It was a bright moonlit night, almost daylight.

Arriving at Windmill Lodge, we were told that the German planes approaching could be bombers or troop carrying planes and all open spaces in the West Country had to be patrolled in case the planes landed. I was detailed to patrol a certain section of the common with a retired Army colonel. At the time we had not been issued with arms, and I was wondering what use we would be, as the only offensive weapon I possessed was a penknife.

As we walked out of the gate on to the common, the retired colonel put his hand on my shoulder and said, "Just a moment laddy." I turned round and in the moonlight, saw him open an overcoat he was wearing, pull out a double-barrelled shotgun, open it, load it with two shells, close the gun and then say, "Right, we'd better be ready for the bastards, laddy." That colonel was quite prepared to take on the might of the German Army with a shotgun and although I don't suppose he would have lasted 30 seconds, I am sure he would have taken quite a few of the enemy with him.

As it happens, that night the German planes did not land on Minchinhampton common and the retired colonel and myself lived on.'

THE WOMEN'S LAND ARMY

'Oddly, no doubt, for a girl living in the industrial north, I joined the Women's Land Army in 1941. I was told to wait for a place at Horticultural College but, anxious to "do my bit", I asked for work in the meantime. This was agreed (the place at college never materialised) and I was told to go to a private house in the Forest of Dean. Out came the atlas to find not only the Forest, but where Gloucestershire was!

There I arrived on a fiercely frosty day in November to find a surly young gardener who, straightaway, handed me a spade and said that we were going to dig up the lawn tennis court! My wonderful landlady packed me off to bed early each evening after a hot bath and with bandaged hands and aches everywhere. Her husband heard the gardener boasting in the local pub that he was going to get rid of me. "We'll see about that!" we said.

When this ordeal was over, he handed me a strange, long-handled implement, pointed to a bed and said, "O it awf." After saying "I beg your pardon" a couple of times and getting the same incomprehensible command, I guessed I had to scrape this thing across the soil to remove the weeds – little realising that I was also taking the tops off all the rhubarb corms. I'm sure the locals enjoyed that story over their pints.

After catching mumps from my hosts' small twins and having

Land Army girls became a familiar sight on Gloucestershire farms – hard but rewarding work.

to spend Christmas in bed, life continued unhappily so I asked to be moved. Lady Bathurst met me in Gloucester and suggested I might be lucky with a job in Prestbury. Land girls had been living here in such appalling accommodation that I would be their last. And so began a blissful four years.'

'In October 1942 I was called up to join the Women's Land Army. My first billet was at Dymock, and having been born and bred in the city of Sheffield, you can guess how different it all was to me. There were four of us in a gang, all from Sheffield. One of the girls I knew and was billeted with all the time and we became very good friends. We were put to work on a threshing machine which went round from farm to farm threshing out the corn for the farmers. At first we all suffered from lots of blisters on our hands as it was very hard work and on our feet from our new boots, which were rather heavy. The farmers and farm workers were very good to us and we always got plenty of tea for the women and cider for the men. Sometimes the farmer's wife would send us out sandwiches or cake, and sometimes we were asked in to share a cooked meal with them, but this was not very often. We only stayed in Dymock for about six months as it was too far for us to travel, then we were moved to billets in the main street in Newent.

For two thirds of the year we worked with the threshing machine, then the rest of the time we went hoeing sugarbeet. I worked on the threshing machine until the end of the war then I went to work on a smallholding helping grow strawberries and tomatoes in the summer and vegetables in the winter. I enjoyed doing this and stayed until April 1948 when I left to marry a local lad.'

'As the train steamed out of Paddington station I leaned out of the carriage window and waved until my mother's figure was no more than a dot on the distant platform. My destination was Stowell Park in Gloucestershire. I had joined the Women's Land Army some months before and at long last I was en route to a new world – an entirely different way of living. Gradually the dark and dusty buildings turned to suburban villas and eventually to green fields and woods. We stopped at the occasional station to pick up a few passengers. No names on any platforms so I began to wonder if I would ever know when my journey had ended.

I sat in my new uniform, cord breeches, green jersey and heavy topcoat with even heavier shoes, and a very fetching felt hat. I felt not a whit self conscious – just so pleased that at long last I had got my own way despite the protestations and tears of my mother. She declared I was throwing away a career of great promise, whereas my gentle Irish father who rarely argued thought I was doing the right thing and so helped to make this one decision that would change my life completely.

After two hours of thinking and wondering I realised the train was slowly steaming to a halt – a long barren platform, with just an elderly porter quietly calling, "Any passengers for Andoversford?" I lugged my heavy cases out of the compartment and stood feeling quite lost. Not another person alighted – not a soul on the platform either. A low thick mist hung everywhere. I was to be met, that I knew, but by whom I was not at all sure. The old porter – I never saw the stationmaster – said he would ring Stowell to say I had arrived, as he couldn't have me freezing to death on his platform!

Eventually a very beautiful woman, tall and elegant, arrived, apologised for being late and led me to a chauffeur driven car and helped load my very battered cases into that superb vehicle. I was told later that my collector was Lord Vestey's daughter.

In silence we drove along empty roads and narrow lanes until eventually we stopped alongside some farm cottages. An elderly woman came to greet us; she and her daughter had been evacuated from North London and had agreed to take two or three land girls as lodgers.

I had a feeling that somehow I was not welcome – but suddenly from out of the shadow of the little hallway emerged another land girl, about my age. She had a broad grin on her face and introduced herself. Audrey had lived in a town and had a mother who spoilt her – like my own, and again like me, she had never left home before. She was to become my greatest and most loving friend.

Those first few weeks introduced us to life in the country with a vengeance. Rising early to rush through the garrison barracks of my home in Woolwich to catch a train to London – being pushed and shoved into buses already full before arriving at the studio where I worked for Lenare, the Court Photographer was not comparable to venturing out into a dark frozen world where

By this personal message I wish to express to you

JOAN EILEEN CARD, W.L.A. NO: 135832

my appreciation of your loyal and devoted service as a member of the Women's Land Army from

4.8.43 *to* 4.10.46.

Your unsparing efforts at a time when the victory of our cause depended on the utmost use of the resources of our land have earned for you the country's gratitude.

Elizabeth R

Land girls received official recognition of their work after the war, as did many others who worked on the Home Front.

brussel sprouts had to be picked with cold wet mittened fingers and potatoes sorted from wet muddy pits in bleak fields high on the Cotswolds. Audrey too, instead of a career as a hairdresser in a warm and expensive salon, had to cycle five miles each day to an isolated farm on the edge of the estate.

We were both determined to stick it out. Our letters home never once mentioned the cold rooms, the unappetising food, the wet clothes never really dried. Somehow our mothers must have guessed because food parcels started to arrive – chocolate, home-made cakes, dried fruit. They spent their precious food coupons on us. Each evening as we opened the cottage door we looked for signs of the postman's visit. As farm workers we were allowed extra cheese and meat. With the dairy right next door we had a plentiful supply of milk, and the hens laid eggs obligingly. Rabbits too were shot and delivered to our doorstep. Despite all this our diet that first year was dull, uninspiring and frugal. Sandwiches were generally two slices of dry bread filled with cold mashed potato and maybe a little cheese. We ate them without complaint, mainly because we were always so hungry, and anyway we were too nervous to protest!

Living on a large estate brought us into contact with the "big house". As our digs lacked a bathroom, we were invited to take a bath each week at Home Farm – a luxury after the cold water ablutions that we hurried through each morning. In the winter months we often didn't bother, for the water in the jug was frozen solid. All the staff were kind to us – I think they realised that our life out of working hours was not quite like home had been. After our baths we sat in the kitchen with the cook and had chicken fricassee and baked apples.

Although the work was hard we loved it. Oliver Leach, the head gardener, made me so welcome and taught me everything he knew. He never became cross if I did anything wrong like cutting rhubarb instead of pulling it! Audrey too had a wonderful boss. He taught her to drive a tractor and to plough. The men on her part of the farm treated her with amusement at first, and then with great respect – she could plough better than any of them! If she was working near the farm the foreman's wife invited her in to sit by the warm range at lunch time. I was never allowed back to my digs and had to eat my sandwiches in the draughty potting shed.

Despite the great change in our way of life, and our diet, we survived. All the men on the farm and in the gardens now accepted us – originally they had said "we wouldn't last long."

Spring and summer came, and with it haymaking and harvesting for Audrey, and for me the planting of potatoes, the picking of soft fruit, weeding a plenty, and then at last the storing of apples and pears and the lifting of the root crops. When winter returned I had become a dab hand at double digging, and Audrey had entered a ploughing match!

After three years Audrey and I moved into a minute cottage of our very own. We had oil lamps and a big range to cook on, and a "privy" across the road – a long way to run on a cold night!

I too had moved, from the gardens to the stables. I became a carter. With one head carter, one boy and four other men I knew I had to prove my worth. As our cottage was nearest to the grazing field it was my job to go with a hurricane lamp to fetch the shire horses in at dawn for their food and grooming. Blossom, an old mare, always led them in; Prince, a great ginger horse, came last – there were twelve in all. I learnt to ride side saddle with just an old sack to cover Blossom's broad back, and another sack to drape around my shoulders if it rained. I learnt to plough and drill, trudging to and fro across the great fields in all winds and weathers, guiding those gentle creatures along the furrow until it was time to return each evening. If the horses were very tired then we walked beside them. Each Saturday the "boy" and I collected the village rubbish to take to the dump. We would harness Prince and set off. Prince had a wicked sense of humour and just as young John tipped the rubbish into the cart Prince would move forward a foot. I never swore, but John, a London cockney evacuee, had a fantastic vocabulary. I learnt a lot from him!

The head carter's family had lived in the village for generations. His wife too came from an old Gloucestershire family. She would invite me in to dry out after a hard day's ploughing. I always sat by an enormous fire and as her "men" sat round the kitchen table to eat I was plied with huge slices of plum duff.'

A Child's War

Children faced a bewildering change in their lives, none more so than the little evacuees who arrived in Gloucestershire from the beginning of the war. Sometimes an unhappy experience, far from home and family, many nonetheless found new homes here, and new friends.

To the Grammar School

'In September 1939 I started at the local grammar school. We had a grammar school from Birmingham evacuated to our school, so in the mornings we had our lessons, and in the afternoon the Birmingham children had theirs. We only had half a day's schooling, but we had to go in on Saturday mornings as well, which was not so good. In the afternoons, when the blackberries were ripe, we were expected to go and pick them. They would be taken to school and made into jam in the school kitchen to help with the food situation. We had to carry our gas masks everywhere, and we made attractive covers for the cases.'

Going Bugging

'Early in the war years I was just starting my teaching career. Jobs were scarce and I was assigned for my first attempt to a class of eight year olds at Badminton school for a month.

It proved to be quite a month with one special highlight. The classroom had a door which opened on to a small garden and the road close to the gates of Badminton House where Queen Mary was staying with the two princesses, Elizabeth and Margaret. Imagine my feelings when this door opened one morning to admit the Queen and her grand-daughters, with the request for me to let her have six girls to go "bugging" in the gardens of Badminton House. That, she explained, was picking off slugs and snails. Luckily the headmaster appeared and permission was given.'

A Passion for Bears

'When the Second World War started, I was a small child with a passion for teddy bears.

It was considered necessary for everyone to be issued with gas masks, which they were obliged to take with them wherever they went. The chairman of the local parish council came to our house one evening, for us to try on gas masks for size. I was terrified, and refused to have this strange thing with a peculiar smell over my face.

Then the air raid siren sounded, and we all dived under our sturdy farm kitchen table. We crouched there for some while, until the "all clear" was sounded.

My father solved the problem of persuading me to wear a mask by making a replica for my favourite and oldest teddy, a bear by the name of Jimmie. Father was a keen pipe smoker, and used a round tobacco tin for the snout, with holes pierced in the bottom with a nail. He cut the face covering from a piece of rubber, with tapes to secure it behind Jimmie's head.

This reassured me as, since Jimmie was happy to wear his gas mask, so was I, and, indeed, I often used to play games which required me to wear the once-feared object.'

The Evacuees Arrive

'We had evacuees at Stonehouse, our boy being a really tough, hardened lad from the East End of London whom my gentle mother could not control in any way, so he was rebilleted. My aunt at Chalford, however, had a much sterner disposition and she took all the really difficult cases whom no one else would house. She literally taught them to use a knife and fork – and even a bathroom – before they could go on to other homes. I used to spend all my summers with this aunt, to ease my overworked mother's burden. I remember two evacuees arriving and then being stood on a blanket to catch the fleas whilst their clothes were stripped off and burnt. They screamed blue murder at having to have a bath, which they had never experienced before.'

Holiday at Home

'During the war years Miss Golding, headmistress at Stone with

Woodford primary school, gave up her August holiday and organised a Holiday at Home on the village green with games, races and donkey rides for all the children from Stone, including evacuees from Harwich.'

I CAME TO GLOUCESTERSHIRE

'We three children of the Pugh family, Bill aged eleven, Alf aged nine, and Margaret aged seven, were evacuated to Gloucestershire from Lozells Street school, Birmingham, on 3rd September 1939. The evacuation started with a walk to Hockley Wharf where we all entrained. Most of us looked real urchins because of our shabby clothing which was either darned or patched. In our case our extra clothing was packed into pillowcases. We were all wearing labels in case of getting lost, and had our gas masks over our shoulder. Though the journey has been referred to as traumatic, it was sheer delight to us "townies" seeing so much wonderful countryside. Upon reaching our destination at Tibberton, we were taken inside the school for selection by the locals who had so kindly volunteered to foster us. As I remember it, we were in the centre of the room whilst they walked around us choosing who they wanted. Sort of a cattle market.

My brother Bill and I were chosen along with two other boys. Unfortunately we were separated from our sister, because, as we understood it, a girl was better not living with boys.

We looked aghast at "our" new home. It was very big and was reached up a long gravelled path. There was a large lawn, big gardens, orchard etc and servants. I remember how kind the cook was to us, also the maid, "Minnie". They had a lot of time for us. Madam also spent time with us. On arrival we were all bathed in a hip-bath, but afterwards used an elegant bathroom, of which I think there were three. The beds were luxurious, the sheets smelled wonderful and fresh. Madam always gave each of us a sweet before saying goodnight. Oh yes, we also had pyjamas! Madam herself darned our jumpers and socks. Unbelievable. It was only a short time before new clothes were bought for us and we felt like little Lord Fauntleroys. We lived in the servants' part of the house but often visited the more stately rooms.

Every once in a while our Mom and sister came to see us on a special coach laid on from Birmingham. We would walk to

Barber's Bridge to meet them. Once, when we were expecting to see them, they failed to show up. Other parents told us that "they hadn't seen them and that there had been a heavy bombing raid on Birmingham that night." However, we need not have worried as they had only overslept.

We must have been a worry to our foster-parents, as I recall having a broken arm, ring-worm, putting an axe into my wrist, and I also nearly drowned. Those are just the health problems I remember!

My brother returned to Birmingham in 1942 having reached the working age of 14. By that time the majority of evacuees had returned home for one reason or another. One, I remember, had tried walking it to Birmingham, but was picked up on the far side of Gloucester. I guess some of the children weren't as lucky as us.

Two bombs were dropped in the vicinity where we lived. That was about all we knew of a war going on except for being told, "do not talk to any strangers, as they might be German fifth columnists."

In 1943, I returned home to spend the last few months of my schooling in Birmingham. Evacuation was an experience that I wouldn't have wanted to miss, and I owe a debt of gratitude to the wonderful people of Gloucestershire. They still hold a place in my heart.'

'My sister and I lived in a modern, comfortable house on the outskirts of a large town, some twelve miles from the centre of London and we both attended the local high school. When the war was about to break out and it was decided that all schools in the area should be closed and the pupils sent away, with their teachers, to safer places, we had to close up our home, not knowing when or if ever we were likely to see it again.

At that time, children were not used to travelling about as the children of today do. Most of the children had ventured no farther than a few streets away from their homes and none of them would have left their families before. We all had to meet at a London station to wait for a very long steam train to take us to an unknown place. It remained a secret until we got there. The railway platform was covered by rows and rows of children, from the age of five years upwards and dressed for the colder weather in thick short trousers or skirts, jumpers and jackets, school caps and berets and each carrying a waterproof coat and a case. Each child's name and address had been clearly printed on the labels that fluttered from cases and jackets. Some of the children, especially the little ones, were very frightened. Because I was 17, I was put in charge of a compartment full of five year olds, most of whom were in tears. We sang and told stories until, one by one, they cheered up, with the exception of one little girl who cried throughout the entire journey. Her mother had given her a parting gift of a small bag of boiled sweets and she sat on my lap sucking them. The more she cried the more she sucked, until her face was wet and sticky and all the colours of the rainbow.

A long train journey brought us into Gloucestershire and all of us in the fifth and sixth forms duly arrived in the very pretty village of Redmarley D'Abitot. My sister and I were billeted together in a tiny cottage and our hosts were expecting to house two toddlers. They were astonished to find that they had two teenagers and so were we when we discovered that a tiny little bed and a cot had been prepared for our use. I seem to remember spending a very uncomfortable and precarious night, clinging to my sister and trying not to fall off the under-sized bed. The next day the billeting officer arrived with a larger bed and we were able to get some sleep. Our hosts were very kind to us and we grew quite fond of each other but I don't think that my sister and I ever came to terms with the sanitary arrangements that existed in outlying country districts at that time.

When we first arrived, the vicar came to welcome us. He opened his garden and gave us lemonade and buns. The highlight of the week came on Saturdays, when we all took the bus into Ledbury for the weekly shopping expedition. I never failed to marvel at the patience of the drivers on the return journey who would hold up their buses and wait until the last passenger in the butcher's queue had been served. The bus drivers in my home town were not nearly so obliging. Once we went to the cinema in Ledbury. It was a very small hall with rather quaint seating arrangements. The cheapest seat was a little space on a crowded wooden form, the unfortunate viewers on either end falling off from time to time during the performance. By paying a little extra, we enjoyed relative comfort on a slatted park bench, with curving iron sides and painted white, in front of a row of potted palm trees, which decorated the back of the hall.'

TOWARDS PEACE AT THE KING'S SCHOOL

'The summer term of 1945 saw an optimistic King's School already experiencing some of the benefits which peace was to bring. At Easter senior pupils were allowed to return to what were then the school's main classrooms in Gloucester at the end of Pitt Street. Built in 1929, this block had been requisitioned by the army in 1940, for the billeting first of evacuees and later of the Pioneer Corps. For most of the war the school had suffered extremely cramped conditions. Older boys were taught in "Big School" (now the gym), where the various classes were separated by three curtains, and in the cathedral library.

1945 saw the first school lunches at King's. They were provided for 50 boys from the country districts by the LEA's kitchen at Frampton-on-Severn and were eaten in a Nissen hut built by the army at the back of the Pitt Street classroom block. Boys were asked to bring their own cutlery because of wartime shortages.

The menus became the subject of great curiosity as rationing was gradually relaxed. Once when a mother asked her small boy what he had eaten, he replied, "I don't know; it was pink with white all round" – the first ham he had ever seen! When the pudding was blancmange with pineapple chunks, a boy reported that he did not know what it was, "but the headmaster had eaten his, so it must be alright."

Some thought that the war had had negative effects on the behaviour of the boys at King's. Many were preoccupied with "war games", competing with each other to imitate machine guns or fighter aircraft. On one occasion the Bishop was almost knocked to the ground by a crowd of small boys rushing out of the chapter house and along the cloisters with arms outstretched thinking themselves to be a squadron of Spitfires flying in perfect formation. Other wartime pranks included climbing up the external look-out ladders on the cathedral tower and scrounging chewing gum from American convoys which stopped in Archdeacon Street.

At last by 1945 life was beginning slowly to return to normal, the worst of the war being over for the civilian population. A full programme of athletic sports was held at King's and won by Serlo House. Games had been difficult to organise at King's earlier in the war. In addition to restrictions on transport,

Gloucester Docks.

problems were compounded by the army taking over the paddock for military use. Anti-aircraft guns and two barrage balloons were positioned there surrounded by barbed wire. There was a trench system between Paddock House and Finch's which the school had to use when the air-raid siren sounded. Another part of the paddock was turned over to the cultivation of potatoes. Football was played at Longford, but severe flooding in 1941 washed the goal posts away.

The school's association with the cathedral had no doubt served as a focus for inspiration in the dark days of the war. School prayers were held in the Lady Chapel three days a week.

The choristers were often invited to Badminton to sing for Queen Mary. One boy, dressed in his best school suit, ran down a corridor there out on to what he thought was a lawn, only to end up in two feet of green scum. The Queen made a special point of enquiring into the boy's state when she joined the choristers for tea!'

HIGH DAYS & HOLIDAYS

Highdays & Holidays

Whether it was sports or dancing, we made sure we enjoyed ourselves in those days before television. Every village seemed to have "something going on" and the home-grown talent to make it enjoyable. Then times changed, and "pop music" brought new pleasures for the young.

Winter and Summer

'Between the wars Falfield had a football team, a cricket team and a tennis club. Indoor games such as darts and cribbage were played in the Huntsman House. Plays, dances and socials were organised regularly throughout the winter months at both the village hall and church schoolroom. There was great excitement when the "Lantern Lectures" were held.'

Balls at the George

'I have great memories of the George Hotel in Newent. A very

Stone cricket team in 1935.

Members of Fairford Tennis Club in 1927, when many villages had their own tennis courts.

Victorian property, it hosted many a party and charity ball, including the first Young Farmers' Club dance in 1944.

The ballroom with its open fires witnessed many a posthorn gallop and those underneath in the billiard room certainly knew all about it. Everything stopped when the 18 to 20 stone of Uncle Percy entered the room!'

THE VILLAGE HOP

'I was born and brought up in Cotswold villages from the 1920s. Our youthful dancing was so different from today, yet I am sure enjoyed equally as much – perhaps even more so. We could walk or cycle alone along unlit country roads and lanes in safety, without fear.

Pierrots were popular in concert parties in the 1920s; this troupe performed at Chalford Hill.

For us there was a sort of circuit of dances held in the surrounding hill villages: Dowdeswell village hall; the hut at Withington; Shipton Oliffe reading room; Brockhampton and Whittington halls and the Red Triangle hut at Chedworth.

My first introduction to the "village hop" (as village dances were known) was at Dowdeswell, advertised locally by hand-written posters announcing: "Whist Drive & Dance, 7.30 pm."

My mother was fond of playing whist and would say to me, "There is a whist drive and dance at Dowdeswell next Friday. If you walk there with me (some two miles), I will stay on for a little while for the dance." This was the carrot!

I was about twelve years old when I first went along with Mother; of course I soon met up with other village lads and lassies, who, like me, having no interest in whist, amused ourselves whilst our parents enjoyed the card playing. This was conducted in comparative silence, interrupted occasionally by the MC loudly announcing which cards were trumps, or for players to change tables, also frequent shouts to us youngsters for being over exuberant.

At the end of the whist, scores were checked, winners

announced and prizes presented. This was the time we had waited for. Tables were folded and stacked away, chairs pushed back around the sides of the hall. Cloths were removed from the long tables at the end of the hall, revealing home-made refreshments of all kinds; sandwiches, cakes and tarts (one penny each). Home-made lemonade was poured from large washstand type jugs, the tops of which were covered over with muslin edged with coloured beads; teapots brimming full, all served by a team of ladies from the village. Everyone tucked in!

Dowdeswell, like Chedworth, was rather more fortunate than the other villages because they both had a village brass band, and some members from the band would play the music for dancing.

Music at the other village dances was supplied by gramophone, mostly of the wind-up type; this got quite interesting when the operator was distracted and forgot to wind the handle, the music gradually getting slower and slower, until shouts from the dancers brought him like a bolt from the blue, to frantically wind and wind the handle to revive the rhythm.

At Dowdeswell, during the interval after whist, the three or four musicians would arrive and trundle in with drums, cornet, trombone and bass, and prepare to supply the music for dancing. I can still picture quite clearly in my mind the figure of Joe Broad, the bandmaster of Dowdeswell brass band (who was later to teach me to play), on the raised platform at the end of the hall puffing away on cornet or trombone to the tunes of the waltz, foxtrot or quickstep. Mums and dads, young and old, would be whizzing round the floor, coat tails flying, dancing their own particular style.

I was taught to dance by my mother's friend, Mrs Adams, rather a large lady with a vice-like grip, with me, tangle-footed, being dragged around the floor to the sound of her calling, "Now, one-two-three, one-two-three," trying to teach me the steps in waltz-time. Yes, she taught me and many others. The only lessons we ever had, and for which I have always been grateful.

As soon as I had attained a reasonable standard of dancing, I quickly escaped my tutor's clutches, to dance with the village girls.

As we got a little older, how we looked forward to "the village hop". For many it was a Friday or Saturday night quick dip in the tin bath in front of the living room fire, with a bar of Lifebuoy soap (no posh scented body lotions or shampoos); the bath water perhaps already second or third hand! Getting dressed quickly; hair well greased down with a good dollop of Brylcream, by the light of the table oil lamp.

Now all prepared, next to get the bike out of the shed, and for many of us, after struggling to light our cycle acytelene or oil lamp, meeting up with friends and cycling off together several miles to a "village hop".

Wartime saw village halls packed with dancers, servicemen and women, British and Americans who brought with them the new dances of jive and jitterbug as well as nylon stockings, a new type of chewing gum and Lucky Strike fags. A new up-beat rhythm was introduced, which, at first, stretched the ability of local musicians; but with new records on the old gramophones, great fun was had by all.

The end of the war saw the decline of the village whist drive and dance. For the young a new type of music and dance was being born – together with a changed lifestyle for most.'

SATURDAY EVENINGS

'On Saturday evenings, the place to go was the Gloucester Guildhall dances. The ballroom had a maple-sprung floor, which was wonderful for dancing, especially those long slides in the foxtrot and tango – if you were lucky enough to have a good male lead. Many functions were held at the Guildhall, but it did not have a bar, hence in the interval there was a surge to either the New Inn in Northgate Street or the Saracen's Head in Eastgate Street. The New Inn, a former coaching inn, had a wide entrance and interior features to match, including a courtyard. Functions were presided over by the Guildhall custodian, Eddie Parsons, who was also the City Mace Bearer on formal civic occasions. There was rarely even a slight disturbance, and certainly nothing which needed a police presence; in fact, many of the younger police attended the dances in mufti.

Another venue was the Technical College in Brunswick Road – again no bar, but such facilities were not deemed a "must". At all there was "live" music, requests were played, and the atmosphere was friendly and easy, but no one overstepped the mark of decency having consumed too much alcohol, and the now universal canned beer was unknown.

A third hall with a good floor for dancing was Cheltenham Town Hall (French chalk and all). But rather a problem was getting there and more important getting back to Gloucester. The train service to St James' station with its first and second-class waiting rooms was vital. The railway fare was 1s 6d return, as it was a cheap evening fare, and we bought our own dance tickets at the door for 3s 6d. The problem was that the last train left at 10.45 pm and the dances ended at 10.30 pm. No long passionate leave-taking of a dancing partner, but a frantic dash for the train, after you had begged the cloakroom attendant to "hurry up". The guard was often Ernie Moulder – even when Mayor of Gloucester he enjoyed "chivvying" the late-comers. The rail guard had usually worked the train to Cheltenham earlier and always made sure he brought the same people back. Frantic blowing of the guard's whistle, and the threat to leave expedited the scamper along the platform, though the train had been known to leave a few minutes late if a tired dancer was hobbling along in stockinged feet carrying two high heeled shoes. No female passenger was left behind; also it was a polite and practical way of relieving oneself from a possibly too ardent dancing partner. Few of us had phones and we seldom parted with our address. Upon our return to Gloucester we walked home from the Great Western station with no worries or hassle. Sometimes we met a person exercising a dog, but usually it was a peaceful ending to the week.'

THE ALLIGATOR

'"The Alligator" – an animal as old as Bill Haley and rock and roll itself. The name came from the great Bill Haley hit *See you later ....* and it was about then the club first saw the light of day – or dim light, would be more appropriate – as a private party.

So successful was the party that the next month the club was born (1957) with the latest records and a small skiffle group, better known as The Beatniks.

Once a month the night club held in Taynton and Tibberton village hall, not far from Gloucester, made its impact upon its members and guests with a visiting group in addition to the resident group. Incredible though it may seem, the Beatniks had their rehearsal "pad" in stables belonging to the rectory of the

'Phone 4285 10, PROMENADE, CHELTENHAM

ROBERTSON & Co.

(T. R. Pritchard, Proprietor)

TOBACCONISTS

Cigar and Cigarette Importers

Established 1895

Gloucestershire County Cricket Club

OFFICIAL SCORE CARD. PRICE 3d.

WAGON WORKS GROUND

GLOUCESTER

LET THE CHELTENHAM & GLOUCESTER BUILDING SOCIETY HELP YOU BUY YOUR HOUSE

HERE is a speedy service with no annoying formalities. A sound society with nearly 9 millions of Assets, and an unrivalled Reserve Fund. Why not ask for particulars at once-?

Head Office : Clarence Street, CHELTENHAM
Branches : Tudor House, Westgate Street, GLOUCESTER
also HEREFORD, OXFORD and BOURNEMOUTH

"Thank goodness for Cricket . . . and Cavendish House . ."

CAVENDISH HOUSE of CHELTENHAM. Established 1818

Rationing was still in force in 1946 and spectators at the county cricket match were asked to bring their own refreshments.

neighbouring parish, Highnam.

Annual subscription to the Alligator was 2s 6d a year and every candidate for admission had to be over 14 years of age. One of the club's objectives was to generally try to make local life a bit more cheerful but rules stated, "Every candidate, of whatever age, must agree that there is a subtle difference between having a good time and raising a riot." Ballet star Antoinette Sibley, Derek Hart of television's *Tonight* and two Bishops visited the club, not forgetting M.P. Price, MP for the Forest of Dean, whose son Peter played a leading role in the success of the venture.

So with soft lights and hot music you never quite knew who you would meet at the bar or dancing in front of the stage. Sadly, times changed, riots were raised and the Alligator closed in 1971.'

TUFFLEY ROVERS AFC

'The founding meeting of Tuffley Rovers AFC took place in a railway coach in the summer of 1929. The coach came from Grange Court railway station in March 1925 and remained in the Stroud Road opposite Tuffley post office for a good 30 years. It was the home and workplace of Donald Hall, a remarkable man brought up in a boys' home at Tuffley Court, who became a boot and shoe repairer. The coach was a mecca for Rovers players and their followers, who usually on a winter's night would enjoy the cosiness of the venue whilst conducting an inquest into the previous game.

George Whitfield, owner of Robinswood Brick and Tube Company was a great admirer of Donald's business enterprise and ability. When Donald tactfully enquired about the possibility of a loan to launch the new football club, Mr Whitfield was only too delighted to help.

There were differences about the colours: some wanted to play in the Villa colours whereas others liked the red and white coloured design of Arsenal. Eventually a compromise was reached – the colours would be the claret and blue of Villa but the shirt design that of Arsenal.

As for a ground to play on, Donald had negotiated the lease of a field, "Moss Field", on Tuffley Lane alongside the railway line. Changing quarters were a room at the cottage on the ground with hot water and the laundering of the towels provided by Mrs Moss – all free of charge.

The club finished third in the League at the end of its first season, with a credit of £6 4s 11d, thanks to whist drives and a Married v Single football match. In the semi final of the Stroud Hospital Junior Cup our opponents were none other than Tuffley YMCA! I remember the game as though it were yesterday – a bad tempered bruising "derby" played at Sutgrove (now pitches for Carlton Road school) before a large and very partisan crowd. A couple of players were sent off and we were beaten. But the gate was easily a record then, for any Junior Cup Semi Final, amounting to no less than £7 10s 0d.

Our changing quarters in 1932 were the garage at "The Owls", 8 Grange Road which belonged to the club trainer, Percy Andrews. There in Percy's garage, both home and visiting teams changed. The hot water was supplied from an old brick-built furnace which had a zinc boiler heated by a wood and coal fire. There were two long zinc baths – one for each team – which meant, of course, that on a wet and muddy day, those who bathed last had the greatest difficulty in finding the water!'

When the Beatles Came to Gloucester

'The Beatles' connections with Gloucestershire are not well catalogued. They certainly played at the Lydney Town Hall in 1962, commanding a fee of £32 to travel in their van from Liverpool. The audience was unimpressed.

They fared better at the Stroud Subscription Rooms, where their unfamiliar style was received with slightly more enthusiasm.

On 18th March, 1963, the Regal Theatre in King's Square, Gloucester, hosted a pop package show headed by two American stars, Tommy Roe and Chris Montez. Bottom of the bill were The Beatles.

By this time, under the management of Brian Epstein, they sported pudding basin haircuts and chocolate brown suits with round collars. But, as an aspiring bass player and most junior *Citizen* reporter, I was taken with their music – original, vocally harmonic and based on the black rhythm and blues of the late Fifties.

The Beatles closed the first half of the show to an enthusiastic

OFFICIAL PROGRAMME

3d.

Gloucestershire Rugby Football Union

Lancashire Rugby Football Union

Gloucestershire v. Lancashire

KINGSHOLM, GLOUCESTER. SATURDAY, APRIL 26th, 1947

Kick-off 3-30 p.m.

OUR VISITORS

We welcome to-day, Lancashire, whom we first met at Manchester on March 14th, 1891, when we suffered defeat by 4 goals, 2 tries, to nil! thus Lancashire proving County Champions for that season. We next met them at Liverpool (Blundellsands) on March 8th, 1930, and reversed the decision, winning by 13 points to 7, we thus becoming Champions for that season. The next time we had the pleasure of meeting Lancashire was on April 12th, 1947. when, as you are aware, the match resulted in a draw - 8 points each, thus causing to-day's re-play. This is, therefore, the first opportunity we have had of welcoming our visitors to Gloucestershire.

The programme for the Gloucs v Lancs rugby union replay match in 1947.

but hardly maniacal audience of 1,200. Later, during top of the bill Chris Montez' performance of *Let's Dance*, a girl from Tetbury tried to get on to the stage and fell heavily into the orchestra pit. She was helped out by the American star and taken away for treatment.

On the pretext of inquiring after her health, I went round to the New County Hotel in Southgate Street, where the bands were staying. Montez was in the dining room and gave me a good line about sending the girl a bouquet of flowers. As we were talking, two figures approached from the next table.

They announced they were Beatles, had a record out called *Love Me Do* and any publicity would help. I inquired as to their names and was told, "I am Paul McCartney and this is John Lennon." How do you spell McCartney? He wrote it down in my notebook.

If only I had kept that notebook! Within a couple of months the Beatles were top of the charts, household names and the hottest property in showbusiness. The rest is history.'

RADIO AND CINEMA

The radio was part of the family, enlivening many an evening round the fire for children and adults alike. Going to the local cinema came to be a weekly (at least!) delight and how sad it was when so many of our favourite venues disappeared as television lured us away.

RADIO IN THE 1940S

'In the corner of our gas-lit living room was a recess which contained our Lissen wireless, with its significant name on the front. The rectangular case, open at the back, contained delicate glass valves, a loudspeaker, tuner and other mysteries as well as space for a box-shaped Exide high tension battery. It had small sockets into which wires tipped with red and black plugs were inserted. Alongside stood a tall, square glass-cased accumulator with a carrying handle and knobs on the top into which wires were inserted and contacts made with the set.

The central knob on the set moved a pointer allowing tuning in to various stations but stayed usually at the BBC Home Service. Wires encased in cotton trailed round the room and through a hole in the window frame to the outside aerial and earth. The *Radio Times* delivered weekly was kept in an embroidered folder on the top of the set.

As with other Forties items, listening was rationed, to conserve battery power. We could listen to *Children's Hour* – Toytown stories were favourites – and Uncle Mac always ended with "Goodnight children, everywhere." Wartime news bulletins were heard in silence, with glances at the map on the wall to identify places mentioned. At 6.45 pm came escapism – the music of *Coronation Scot* heralded *Dick Barton, Special Agent,* never to be missed. If we were home at lunchtime, there would be *Workers' Playtime* from a canteen somewhere in England. Wilfred Pickles' programme *Have a Go* marked a watershed in the change from BBC English to regional accents. *ITMA* was not to be missed, nor the King's broadcast at 3 pm on Christmas Day.

At lunchtime on Saturday, my errands concluded, I would be sent to lug the heavy accumulator to the garage. Having waited seemingly for ages, someone would bring the other one then fully charged, I would pay sixpence and carry the charged one home. Once connected to the set – why was it called a "wireless" with so many wires? – Father could listen to the football results and later we all sat round to listen to *Saturday Night Theatre,* after *In Town Tonight.* Alas, sometimes the sound faded right away – the high tension battery had run out and we would never know "whodunnit". A new one was expensive and difficult to track down. We did indeed "Lissen" to our wireless, a focal point in our lives.'

Better Than the Magic Lantern

'At Charlton Kings we went to the "pictures" once a year at the end of the summer holiday. The silent films were playing then, but they were better than the old magic lantern, cranked by hand. A piano played throughout the film to create the atmosphere – especially when the heroine was tied to the railway line.'

Wotton Cinema

'Wotton cinema was started in 1913 by the owners of the old Crown Inn in Market Street, which had closed in 1911. The Crown Inn had large premises and the upstairs banqueting room was converted to house the cinema.

The cinema operated on gas and the great surge of gas which it used when it started made the lights go down in Market Street which caused a lot of consternation. Later electricity was used and in the 1940s teenagers were employed to crank the motor and keep the belt running.

In spite of such operating difficulties, the cinema was well attended and in 1931 when sound was introduced there was a boom year – until sound was introduced at Dursley in 1932. Rivalry has always existed between the neighbouring towns of Dursley and Wotton and in 1932 Dursley caught up and the boom died down. In 1921 the cinema had moved downstairs where a special extension had been built to house it, but the apertures through which the films were shown remained in the large top room until the old Crown Inn was eventually demolished and a new building replaced it.

I remember attending the cinema in my school days in the 1940s. The proprietor was rather deaf so he didn't always get the sound right – either it was deafeningly loud or you couldn't hear it at all. When this happened the audience would stamp their feet and whistle and then the proprietor's wife would come out and clap her hands and shout at everybody to be quiet, "especially those at the grammar school" – we were always the worst. Meanwhile the film went merrily on and we had to follow it the best way we could.

The price of the seats ranged from 2s 3d at the back on plush padded seats, through 1s 9d halfway down which were not quite so plush, to the front seats which were ordinary wooden chairs at 9d. The very front row was 6d. The back seats were always coveted by courting couples and the front ones were usually occupied by children who could only afford 9d or 6d out of their meagre pocket money. We took my uncle there one night when he was staying with us on holiday and the film showing was *The Magic Bow* with Stewart Grainger. Just as the film was coming to a romantic climax someone rolled a beer bottle down the aisle. As the aisle had wooden slats going across it, the bottle made an awful noise but it amused my uncle greatly as he was rather fond of his drink and he kept chortling all the way home.

The cinema kept running until the 1960s. It had two other proprietors after the first ones and one of the teenagers who operated the motor in the 1940s took it over in 1962. It closed in 1965 when all cinemas were at their lowest ebb, but has recently reopened.'

A Regular Treat

'A regular treat in my childhood was the trip to the pictures. For 1s 9d you could enjoy two films, a newsreel and trailers of forthcoming attractions. In fact, if you wished you could on a Saturday go into the cinema when it opened, sit through all the repeats and come out after "God save the King". All for 1s 9d. As more and more people bought televisions the little local cinemas gradually closed.'

Last Days of the Hippodrome

'On the evening of Sunday, 23rd October, 1955 fire broke out at the Hippodrome cinema in Eastgate Street, Gloucester. Before long, the building was enveloped in smoke and flames, but luckily the 1,239 patrons watching *Night Riders of Montana* were able to file out in good order.

A huge crowd gathered in King's Square to watch the building burn, which it did in spectacular fashion. Clouds of smoke billowed into the sky as firemen sought to contain the blaze. The manager, Mr Frank Witts, was later quoted as saying that the Hippodrome always put on a good show!

It was swiftly rebuilt – upstaging the recently-completed Regal cinema in King's Square – and was open for business again on Monday, 18th June, 1956. The reopening ceremony was performed by the Mayor of Gloucester, Alderman M.G. Lewis and the British actor, Trevor Howard. The film chosen to relaunch the Hippodrome was the Rodgers and Hammerstein musical *Carousel*, shot in Cinemascope 55. The auditorium was completely modernised, with 1,400 seats and a purple carpet especially woven for the cinema.

In April 1959 the Hippodrome was renamed the Gaumont. Then came rumours of city centre redevelopment. The cinema closed its doors on 22nd April, 1961. Its last double programme was *Murder Incorporated* and *Desire in the Dust*. But it stayed empty for another three and a half years until September 1964, when demolition work began.

The Hippodrome was not the first city cinema to go up in smoke. That honour goes to the Theatre de Luxe in Northgate Street, which was gutted on 30th January, 1939.'

ROYAL CELEBRATIONS

From the beginning of the century, towns and villages across Gloucestershire have celebrated royal coronations and jubilees with enthusiasm. The Queen's coronation in 1953 was different from those that had gone before – by the magic of television we were able to watch the ceremony itself.

REJOICING SINCE 1900

'Wyck Rissington has rejoiced in the monarchy throughout the years. In 1900 there was public rejoicing with sports, teas and patriotic songs on the green to commemorate the successes of the Queen's forces in South Africa, and especially the capture of Pretoria. An effigy of President Kruger was dragged along in a procession – his beard was shaved off and he was relieved of his tall hat – and burnt on the bonfire. (Forty-five years on, on VE Day, an effigy of Hitler was to suffer the same fate.) A year later a special service was held to commemorate the passing of "our late beloved Queen".

A day of celebration on Coronation Day 1911 began with a gale of wind which laid the marquee prostrate and all efforts to re-erect it proved in vain. So 120 sat down to dinner in a smaller tent and the health of His Majesty King George V was proposed, then that of Queen Alexandra, the Prince of Wales and the Royal Family. The bonfire and a splendid display of portfires and rockets was spoilt only by the rain. As many as 37 bonfires could be seen from Wyck Beacon on the hills around.'

JUBILEE AND CORONATION IN THE 1930S

'For George V's Jubilee in 1935 all the children at Coopers Hill received a silver medal of commemoration from the MP, Mr Robert Perkins, who came in person to deliver them. I seem to remember a tea party down in the old barn adjacent to the Pound Farm – long trestle tables absolutely laden with food of all kinds. I remember especially the huge cream puffs! When you ate one you got cream all over your nose and cheeks, but my, they tasted good.'

'When George VI's Coronation celebrations took place at May Hill, the children were very patriotic and wore Union Jack aprons for the tea party! There were Coronation mugs for all the children and spoons for those lucky enough to win the sporting events. In the evening there were jollifications on May Hill.'

THE QUEEN'S CORONATION 1953

'As a child of eight years old I was living with my parents in one of the gate houses on the Lodge Park estate of Lord Sherborne. I don't remember the announcement on 6th February 1953 of the death of King George VI, however I do remember that shortly

An ox-roast was held at Fairford in 1937 to celebrate George VI's coronation.

afterwards my parents started paying 6d per week to a fund in the local village of Aldsworth. This was to contribute towards a celebration to be held on 2nd June 1953 for the coronation of Queen Elizabeth II.

Although the weather was not perfect on 2nd June all those who participated from the village and surrounding areas thoroughly enjoyed the celebrations. As children we were not, of course, conscious of all the work that had gone into the organisation of such an event, we just enjoyed ourselves. The celebrations took place in the large hangar-like sheds that normally housed the Marchants Coaches based in Aldsworth. These were all cleared out, the sheds cleaned and trestle tables piled high with food.

A number of events made the day stand out in my memory. What most children remembered was that we were presented with a Coronation mug, which I wish I still had, and two ice cream tokens. This was certainly one of the highlights of the day as ice cream was something most of us children had not previously experienced.

It was not only a memorable day because of the Coronation of Queen Elizabeth but it was also the first time that I, and indeed most of the others in the village, had seen a television set. There was only one cottage in the village that had a television and I remember my parents being invited along with myself and my sister into the cottage to see part of the Coronation as it happened. It was a far cry from the slimline, large screen television sets of today. It was a floor standing model about three feet in height and about 15 inches wide. The screen was quite small but had a recognisable black and white picture. There was a feeling of unreality and almost disbelief to be actually watching an event which was taking place over a hundred miles away. Very different from hearing it described on the radio and imagining what everything looked like.'

'I was living in a prefabricated bungalow in Tewkesbury. Only one neighbour had a television but everyone in the road was invited to watch, so it was quite a crush.'

'Afterwards, for such a small village as Arlingham, we deemed the day to have been a huge success. A committee had been formed; it met several times and I wrote copious notes, being happy to be appointed honorary secretary (treasurer too, I guess, because I well remember organising a house to house collection to obtain funds).

Rationing had not long ended and many types of food were still scarce or unobtainable. Yet we were determined to have a tea for all villagers who cared to come to the village schoolroom. My husband was one of the two contributors towards buying Coronation mugs – one for each child – to be presented after the meal.

The day dawned more like a day in November, with misty rain, a chilly wind and an exceedingly cold temperature for early June. Most disappointing! During the earlier part of the morning a crowd gathered on the Cross and I sat outside the (then) post office with my notebook of minutes to make sure all went well. It all went very well, except the weather!

There was no time to lose because we all wished to be by our radios or TV sets. Mains electricity was not thought of in 1953. It did not arrive in the village until 1955 (summer) so only those of us with our own little engines chugging away in an outside shed or outhouse were able to have the luxury of television. In 1951 we were the first household to buy a set. The tube failed just after the guarantee ran out. A major disaster! By 1953 I believe there were three sets in the village – we obviously held supremacy because on each Saturday afternoon my living room was invariably full of a motley audience of old men, invited by my husband, to watch the football matches. They thought it to be some kind of magic which, never in their wilder dreams, had they anticipated!

But, this day was something really special. I'm quite sure our visitors were not invited – but they came, all the same, assured of a welcome. How pathetic that small black and white set would appear today. Yet it was then quite wonderful. I think I managed to see a good proportion of the ceremony between constantly putting the kettle on to the old gas stove in the kitchen to supply the assembled company with cups of tea!

By early afternoon our room was full to capacity, sitting and standing – so that when our neighbour's relatives turned up from Bristol, all they could do was to peer through the window in an endeavour to catch a glimpse of the Queen.

At tea-time we all made our way to the schoolroom where we found long trestle tables laden with a good selection of food – for what we then called a knife and fork tea. We all ate well.

Then it was all over and we went home to see the Queen appear on the balcony of Buckingham Palace. After a succession of kings it seemed very strange to adjust to the thought of a *queen* – Elizabeth II – the first since Victoria, who had reigned for so long she had become a national institution, and we would have to remember to sing "send *her* victorious".'

THROUGH THE YEAR

Every year brought its calendar of celebration and fun, from fairs to Whit Walks or Club Days.

DAFFODIL SUNDAY

'At daffodil time the Toc H society held Daffodil Sunday at Newent in the 1940s. Pickers from Gloucester and other places cycled out to pick the daffodils and they were asked to pick an extra bunch so they could be sent to London for distribution to the hospitals. The picking of even one bunch of wild daffodils is, of course, now forbidden.'

MOTHERING SUNDAY

'In my childhood days, Mother's Day was known as Mothering Sunday. We always attended Sunday school in the afternoon, but on this day we took our mothers to a special afternoon service. During this we were invited up to the altar, where the vicar was waiting with a big tray of posies of violets. He handed one to each child and we went back to our seats and gave them to our mothers with a kiss. Arriving back home for tea, we children set the table, the centre of attraction being the Simnel cake, specially ordered from the local baker. We had bought this with our own combined pocket money, which was not very much in those days.'

MAY WALKING

'The first Sunday in May was kept for May Walking at Box, with a very early start being made to walk to Rodborough Fort, where the Salvation Army held an open air service attended by people from the Stroud area.

May 13th, "marking day" for the cattle which the local farmers turned out to graze on the common, was the day to plant runner beans. Hopefully, by the time they showed through the ground, the May frosts would be past.

If Whit Sunday was late and there had been a mild spring, spring cabbage was eaten with the new season's lamb, followed by gooseberry pie.'

MAY DAY AND EMPIRE DAY

'May Day, on the 1st of May, was a time for celebration in Wyck Rissington.

"Oh, we'll go Maying together
And out in the meadows roam,
We should not be wasting this weather

May Day celebrations at Stone Green in 1937.

In idle rest at home
So lasses and lads
Get leave of your Dads
And away to the maypole hie."

May garlands were carried round all the farms and the children sang May songs.

Empire Day, on 24th May, was also celebrated, especially by the schoolchildren. The school was decorated with bluebells, red campion and Queen Anne's lace.

A huge Union Jack was broken from the flagpole in the playground, and the children in their best clothes lined up to sing:

"We salute thee and we pray
Bless O God our land today."

Other songs included *The Bluebells of Scotland, Land of my Fathers*, the National Anthem and many others. Later May Day became just another public holiday and Empire Day ceased to be recognised.'

WHIT SUNDAY – BREAD AND CHEESE

'The Bread and Cheese ceremony on Whit Sunday was the highlight of the year in St Briavels. New clothes were specially bought for the day, when you met up with all the family come back for the day. Both pubs would be open, the George and the Crown.

The ceremony was performed each year to confirm the commoners' right to cut their bean and pea sticks from the Hudnalls or take the free wood. The bread and cheese used to be taken into church to be blessed before being thrown, cut into tiny cubes, from the pound wall to the congregation. It was said, if you kept it, it would never go mouldy!'

WHIT MONDAY

'Whit Monday was a big day in our church calendar years ago. It was an annual event when the whole church united to make a public witness in a happy parade around the streets of Minchinhampton, followed by a tea party in the Sunday school.

From early morning, the ladies would be busy in the kitchen cutting sandwiches, sorting cakes and buns and laying out tables for the tea after the parade. We would squeeze as many people in as possible along the trestle tables and long wooden forms. The men would be busy too in the graveyard decorating the floral crown with lilac, golden chain, peonies and any other flowers and greenery brought along. The primary teachers would be busy in the church centre decorating the little cart for the scholar with the most attendances to ride in and making headdresses for the little attendants.

In the afternoon, after a singing practice in the church with Avening Silver Band, everyone gathered outside in the street. The floral crown always headed the procession accompanied by the minister and the Sunday School Superintendent with the band close behind. Next came the most senior members of the Bible Class and church members and the little ones brought up the rear with the youngest baby on the Cradle Roll in its decorated pram.

Our route took us up the street and along by the allotments, down Friday Street to the Market Square where we sang our first hymn, down the High Street and up to the top of West End for another hymn, back down to the Cross and a little way down Well Hill where we always sang "Jesus bids us shine", then back to the Cross to render "All Hail the Power of Jesu's Name" – I remember it well! – then up to Chapel Lane to sing "God Bless Our School" outside in the lane before making our way into the building for tea.

Nearly every room in the building was used that day both upstairs and down. The band had a room of their own for their free tea and the little tots were also downstairs with their little tables and chairs.

The weather was always kind to us – we never got wet – although I can remember heavy showers falling as soon as we all got indoors on a few occasions.

After tea we would all go up to the park for sports and games and the band would play for the enjoyment of the adults. I don't remember how they carried the long wooden forms for the band to sit on but they appeared somehow, and I remember how silly the cows looked when they heard the music – they were quite attracted to it and would gradually move in closer to stand and listen! If you were good enough to win a race you got either 9d, 6d or 3d, and this was spent later at the George Rogers fun fair which always arrived for Whitsun and attracted crowds from all round the district. Folks would walk up from Burleigh, Brimscombe, Chalford, Box and Nailsworth and line the streets to see us first before going on to the fair. We always received a donation from George Rogers who never opened his fair on Whit Monday until we had gone round the town with our parade.'

'On Whit Monday at North Nibley, a man pushed a truck through the woods and set up a stall selling sweets. This was a great treat to us. There was always more fruit available than sweets.'

'We, at St Mary's church, Kingswood Abbey, had a "treat" on Whit Monday, or it may have been Tuesday. I am sure that the sun always shone. We marched around the village with our Sunday school banner which is still in the church beside the altar – we were led by the Abbey Band and we walked as far as Kingswood House where we sat under a glorious willow tree while the members of the band had some liquid refreshment. Then we walked a short distance to Penn House, now a nursing home, and there we had an orange each. Next stop was the Sunday schoolroom for a splendid tea – a delicious cream cake was a wonderful treat in those days.

After tea we ran across the field opposite to Chestnut Park Farm where some of the men had erected a swing – ropes and a strong wooden seat hanging from a stout branch of one of the chestnut trees growing in the field. Some of the trees are still there after 80 years have gone by. We also had races and scrabbles for sweets. I did not benefit from either of these attractions because I was no runner and never won any races – as for scrabbling for sweets I would never have lowered my dignity, even at eight years old – but I loved the march around the village behind the band, the tea served by the ladies of the church and the glorious swings right up into the leafy chestnut trees. Why did it never rain?'

Whit Tuesday Treat

'Whit Tuesday was a red letter day at Kilcot, when we had tea, fun and games in a field kindly lent by a local inhabitant. Teachers from the Sunday school brought mugs, individual bags of buttered buns and sandwiches, and bottles of lemonade to the field, all carried in large tin baths. The greatest fun was finding wrapped sweets in the grass, thrown from a large jar by the teachers.'

ANNUAL CLUB DAY

'One of the red letter days during the early 1900s in the lives of the inhabitants of Sherborne, especially for the children, was the annual Club Day. This joyous occasion was to celebrate the forming of a working men's club, and was always held on Whit Tuesday. Each club member paid a sum of money monthly to the elected secretary/treasurer, who for many years was the late Tom Mathews. The payment ensured that the working man's family would have the service of a doctor free, and a small weekly sick payment should the husband become ill.

Children awoke early on Club Day, all keyed up with excitement. We eagerly awaited the arrival of the show people bringing in their tackle. Living at the bottom end of the village we had the privilege of witnessing these arrivals as they came from Great Barrington where they had been the previous day. I very well remember three Burford families who brought their fair equipment: they were the Forests, the Rowles family and the Bowermans. The event took place in the field behind the school which was clearly visible from our house. We watched all the activity of assembling the swinging boats, roundabouts and marquees; the lads, of course, were on the spot.

About 10.30 am the villagers would assemble at the bottom end opposite Sherborne Farm. At 11 am Chedworth Silver Band, headed by Daniel Large carrying the Union Jack banner, led the procession to the church for a short service. After the service, everyone proceeded back to the war memorial led by the band. Prayers were said by the vicar in memory of the men who had lost their lives during the 1914-1918 war.

At the conclusion of the prayers the male Club members made their way into the school taking their plate, glass and cutlery to partake of a cold lunch of salt roast beef, potatoes, pickles and chutney followed by cheese! All would be washed down with glasses of beer and lemonade (made from fresh lemons) for the lads or teetotallers. The lunch was prepared by a committee of about 18 ladies. The wives and children would make their way home to have a snack lunch.

Sherborne Club Day in 1919, a day out for all the family.

By mid-afternoon the fun of the fair would be in full swing. Screams and shouts of laughter coming from the swing boats where lads tried to outdo each other by swinging their boat higher than their pals, trying to impress their female companions. A continual cry came from the coconut shies with the stallholders enticing the males to "try their luck". There were all kinds of stalls selling toys, coconut ice, brandy snaps, broken wafers, locust beans, sherbet dabs and spit rock. The latter was so-called as it was well known the stall holders who made it from equal quantities of brown and white candy, stretched and plaited together, occasionally spit on their hands during its production. It would set very hard and required breaking with a little wooden mallet before weighing on the old fashioned scales, which had a shallow pan one end and a flat plate the other which held the weights. It was then dropped into a white paper bag.

Races were arranged for the children including running races, three-legged, sack and egg and spoon races. As the field had been grazed by cattle up to Club Day there were lots of cow pats around and inevitably some were unlucky enough to encounter them, necessitating a cleaning up session afterwards.

There were skittles for a case of beer, and bowling into a circle for a live pig (almost every villager reared a pig in those days). There were also bowls for the ladies to win a half tea service. It was a great day for meeting up with friends from neighbouring villages and even from the top end of our own village.

Chedworth bandsmen played all the popular tunes of the time throughout the afternoon and evening in competition with all the noises from the fair. It wasn't surprising that they would occasionally return to the beer tent to quench their thirst.

I always remember those festive days as being gloriously happy, with clear blue skies and lots of sunshine, but in 1910 a severe thunderstorm in the early evening brought the outdoor activities to a sudden close.

The day concluded with a dance (ballroom dancing) taking place in the school until midnight. It was the outbreak of the 1939-45 war which brought this festive day to an end, never to be revived.'

ST BARNABAS FAIR

'Every 11th June at Stone, until the 1970s, Coles fun fair would visit and pitch their caravans. There would be rides such as swing boats and dodgems, and side shows on the village green. They stayed for a week.'

The Wedding Cake entry for Fairford carnival in 1938.

FAIRFORD CARNIVAL

'This was the great event of the year, always held on the second Saturday in July. About 20,000 people would converge on Fairford, and before the war that was a crowd! The carnival raised money for the cottage hospital and there was a wonderful procession of decorated horse-drawn waggons, marching bands, decorated bicycles, prams and pedestrians. The whole procession wound its way round the town before going into the park to be judged. Fairford Carnival was known as "The Best in the West". One year there were 28 marching bands in the procession.'

TIBBERTON FLOWER SHOW

'Someone refers to the third Saturday of August and we automatically think of Tibberton Flower Show. Horticultural shows were popular annual events at the turn of the century and records show that Tibberton's show of 1902 was supported with 450 entries. Although there were few inhabitants, most cottages had a garden of reasonable size which was extensively cultivated to provide food for the family. "Annual Exhibitions", as they were known, were held by the Tibberton, Bulley, Rudford and

Highleadon Horticultural and Industrial Society. The 1914-18 war caused activities to be wound up, but the 1939-45 war encouraged villages to "dig for victory".

Pig Clubs were formed, these being an association of people who clubbed together to purchase pig meal, often at reduced prices. The Tibberton Pig Club decided that as soon as the war was over, they would revive the village horticultural society – which they did – to provide funds for the Tibberton and Taynton Welcome Home Fund for the Rudford and Highleadon Social Club. Tibberton Court, then in use as an old people's home, was the venue for some years.

An ankle competition, darts, driving a nail into a board and "blindman's luck" (cutting down a chicken) were attractions in the 1950s and the hardwood skittle alley made by Ernest Bayliss of Rudford was hired. Those who have lifted it know just how solidly it is made!

Cottagers' classes gradually disappeared and the show grew, grew and grew, and marquees were hired. Entries leapt to 1,130 in 1963 and the *Citizen* described the event as "the show with the most". The most ever home-grown produce had been gathered together for the biggest and best show the society had ever known. In the evening there was a barbecue serving a quantity of chickens and umpteen sausages in record time. Music from The Beatniks and The Castle Jazzmen allowed the visitors to twist the night away – between pillow fights and tug-o-wars. The show was actually announced on the BBC.

Local poet and novelist Laurie Lee wandered among the exhibits in 1968 and was captured on film by chairman Peter Price.

I especially recall visits to Worcester before the big day to collect boxes of reject crockery which we allowed visitors to have the fun of smashing.'

PAINSWICK CLIPPING

'The Clipping Service is held at Painswick in September on the Sunday following the 19th. This is almost a unique ceremony and I hasten to add nothing to do with clipping the yew trees nor to do with clipping sheep. The word derives from an Old English word meaning "to embrace". The origins may well be pagan but it has become a religious ceremony. Revived in Victorian times,

Painswick churchyard.

maybe it was an almost forgotten folk memory. It has been the same now for probably a hundred years.

When I was a little girl we had just the same procession and hymns as we do today. The children wore flowers, usually in a garland round the girls' hair, and a buttonhole for the boys. I can remember the Sunday school teacher poking hair pins into my head to keep the flowers in place. The band played the hymns and round the churchyard went the procession led by our splendid cross, then the choir, then the clergy, the sidesmen and children. Once assembled all round the outside of the church we had the Clipping Hymn, "Daily, daily sing the praises" and all moved forward and back in the chorus, embracing the church, rather in the style of the Hokey Cokey.

Some people used to bake a pie with a china dog inside. Painswick people are sometimes called "Puppy Dogs". One day, it was said, a group of young Stroud men demanded a meal at the Falcon and being short of meat, the landlord made a pie of his puppy dog. When this was discovered great horror and consternation followed and the nickname was first used!'

TEWKESBURY FAIR

'A highlight in the year for Tewkesbury was the Charter Fair each October. The fair was then (in the 1920s) held in all three main streets. The smell of hot traction engines, with their gleaming brass and paintwork, was pervasive. The stalls sold brandy snaps and striped mint humbugs, all sizes. The rides were fewer and simpler – galloping horses, the helter skelter and the cake walk. Then there were the booths challenging local youths to take on the large, muscular fighter and the booths where, if you wished, you could see the lady with two heads!

The marvellous roundabout horses were made in Tewkesbury in Walkers Workshop which was sited on the Oldbury Road.

During the war the fair ceased but the local baker, Billy Wilkins, kept the Charter alive by selling brandy snaps. After the war, back came the fair, and I had the pleasure of seeing my son's delighted face when he saw the lights for the first time after the blackout. Long may it continue to be one of the highlights of Tewkesbury.'

CHRISTMAS TIME

'Christmas was a magical time in Fairford in the 1930s. Edmonds shop in the High Street filled their biggest window with all the delights of childhood – for the girls, dolls, dolls' prams and little tea sets, and for the boys, Meccano, steam engines and small railway sets. The children's presents were paid for out of the Christmas clubs saved at just a few pennies a week, but not everyone could afford to do that and toys had to be bought on Christmas Eve with what money there was left. Edmonds had a large room at the back of the shop which was full of toys at Christmas.'

'We lived in Bishops Cleeve in a big, old farmhouse. All through the year my parents used to pay into a collecting club by putting stamps on their card. Then, before Christmas, a hamper would come containing all sorts of goodies. Once there was a snowy Christmas cake which had a little china house and little carol singers on it. We did love that. If we had anything large to come from town, it came in a carrier's waggon drawn by a large horse. We could hear the sounds of it coming a long way away, and people gathered to see if there was anything for them.'

A NEW YEAR GIFT

'When I was a child, at the beginning of the century, we lived at the bakery at the bottom of Westgate Street, Gloucester. My father, Mr Smith, used to give every child who came to the shop between six and nine o'clock on New Year's morning an orange, a batch cake (a sort of bread roll) and a halfpenny. During the First World War this became a penny, a new one. He continued this custom until 1933.'

INDEX

List of Contributing WIs

Contributions have been received from the following Gloucestershire Women's Institutes:

Almondsbury (Avon) • Amberley • Arlingham • Aschurch
Ashleworth & Hasfield • Aston Keynes (Wilts) • Avening • Blaisdon
Blockley • Box • Broadwell • Brockworth • Bussage & Brownshill • Cainscross
• Cashes Green • Castlegate • Central Cheltenham • Chedworth
Chipping Campden • Churchdown Afternoon • Cinderford • Coaley
Coleford • Coopers Hill • Cranham • Drybrook • Duntisborne Abbots
Dursley • Eastcombe • Elmore • Fairford • Falfield (Avon) • France Lynch
Glevum • Gotherington • Woolstone & Oxenton • Guiting Power • Hampton
Highnam • Huntley • Kilcot & Gorsley • Kingswood Abbey
Newent Lakeside • Lechlade • Leckhampton Evening • Leighterton
Leonard Stanley • Longlevens • Lydney • Maisemore • May Hill
Minsterworth • Moreton Valence • Nailsworth • Newnham upon Severn
North Nibley • Northleach • Norton • Painswick • Prestbury • Priors Park
Quedgeley • St Briavels • Sevenhampton • Sherborne • Shipton Oliffe
Six Ways • Slimbridge • South Cerney • Southam • Southfield
Stanway & Didbrook • Staunton & District • Stone • Tibberton & Taynton
Uckington & Elmstone • Hardwicke • Up Hatherley & The Reddings
Upton St Leonards • Westbury on Severn • Whiteshill & Ruscombe
Willersley • Winchcombe • Woodmancote • Wotton under Edge
Wyck Rissington.